Multistrand Jewelry

Secrets for Success

KALMBACH BOOKS

From the publisher of
Bead Style magazine

Kalmbach Books
21027 Crossroads Circle
Waukesha, Wisconsin 53186
www.Kalmbach.com/Books

Published in 2013
17 16 15 14 13   1 2 3 4 5

Manufactured in the United States of America

ISBN: 978-087116-451-3
EISBN: 978-087116-777-4

The material in this book, with the exception of projects by Naomi Fujimoto on p. 16, 36, 42, and 60, has appeared previously in *Bead Style* magazine or its special issues. Bead Style is registered as a trademark.

Editor: Elisa R. Neckar
Art Directors: Lisa Bergman, Carole Ross
Developmental Editor: Naomi Fujimoto
Technical Editor: Karin Van Voorhees
Illustrator: Kellie Jaeger
Photographers: James Forbes and William Zuback

Library of Congress Cataloging-in-Publication Data
Multistrand jewelry : secrets for success / [compiled by Kalmbach Books ; editor: Elisa R. Neckar].

   p. : col. ill. ; cm.

   "The material in this book, with the exception of projects by Naomi Fujimoto on p. 16, 36, 42, has appeared previously in Bead Style magazine or its special issues"–t.p. verso.
   Issued also as an ebook.
   ISBN: 978-0-87116-451-3

   1. Jewelry making–Handbooks, manuals, etc. 2. Wire jewelry–Handbooks, manuals, etc. 3. Beadwork–Handbooks, manuals, etc. I. Neckar, Elisa R. II. Fujimoto, Naomi, 1970- III. Kalmbach Publishing Company. IV. Title: BeadStyle magazine.

TT212 .M85 2013
745.594/2

Contents

Welcome

Welcome to our collection of multistrand jewelry projects! We know that for new and experienced beaders alike, creating multistrand jewelry can be a challenge, so we've collected a wide array of projects to teach you the skills, tricks, and secrets for successfully creating stunning multistrand necklaces and bracelets. Nearly every project has a unique feature or design twist, so whether you're a beginner or a more experienced beader, you'll find a variety of necklaces and bracelets to suit your skill level and taste; just experiment to find the materials, styles, and techniques you most enjoy.

We hope these projects and their accompanying tips help pave the way to your multistrand success.
Happy Beading!

Naomi Fujimoto
Senior Editor, *Bead Style* magazine

How to Use This Book

Techniques, supplies, and secrets for success are identified at the beginning of every project. Step-by-step instructions with photos will help you make each project. Extra tips and design alternatives are offered as well. Before you get started, you may want to review common techniques, tools, materials, and some helpful hints covered in the next few pages.

SECRETS FOR SUCCESS
Here, you'll find one or more tips from the project's designer, giving you insight into special skills, tricks, ideas, pointers, and the artist's design process.

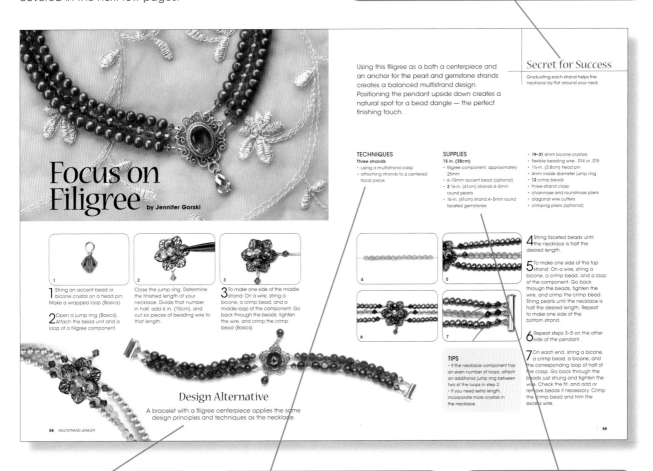

DESIGN ALTERNATIVE
Additional tips about supplies, bead colors, and techniques, as well as suggested alternative ways to create the design, are included in many of the projects.

TECHNIQUES
This summary begins with the number of strands in the piece and continues with the specific techniques you can learn from the project, such as:
- centering a pendant or focal bead
- connecting many stands to a single-strand clasp
- using a multistrand clasp
- using cones to finish a piece
- creating unconventional closures with knots, lariats, and make-your-own clasps
- looping a single strand many times for a multistrand effect

SUPPLIES
This list begins with the length of the bracelet or necklace and also includes a detailed materials list and a list of the tools required to complete the project.

Basic Techniques

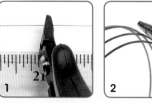

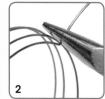

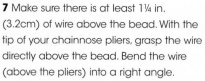

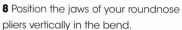

Cutting flexible beading wire

1 Decide how long you want your necklace to be. For a necklace, add 6 in. (15cm) and cut a piece of beading wire to that length. For a bracelet, add 5 in. (13cm).

Cutting memory wire

2 Memory wire is hardened steel, so it will dent and ruin the jaws of most wire cutters. Use heavy-duty wire cutters or cutters specifically designed for memory wire, or bend the wire back and forth until it breaks.

Plain loop

3 Trim the wire ⅜ in. (1cm) above the top bead. Make a right-angle bend close to the bead.
4 Grab the wire's tip with roundnose pliers. Roll the wire to form a half circle.
5 Reposition the pliers in the loop and continue rolling, forming a centered circle above the bead.
6 The finished loop.

Wrapped loop

7 Make sure there is at least 1¼ in. (3.2cm) of wire above the bead. With the tip of your chainnose pliers, grasp the wire directly above the bead. Bend the wire (above the pliers) into a right angle.
8 Position the jaws of your roundnose pliers vertically in the bend.
9 Bring the wire over the pliers' top jaw.
10 Reposition the pliers' lower jaw snugly in the curved wire. Wrap the wire down and around the bottom of the pliers. *This is the first half of a wrapped loop.*
11 Grasp the loop with chainnose pliers.
12 Wrap the wire tail around the wire stem, covering the stem between the loop and the top bead. Trim the excess wrapping wire, and press the end close to the stem with chainnose or crimping pliers.

Making a set of wraps above a top-drilled bead

13 Center a top-drilled bead on a 3-in. (7.6cm) piece of wire. Bend each end upward, crossing the wires into an X.
14 Using chainnose pliers, make a small bend in each wire to form a right angle.
15 Wrap the horizontal wire around the vertical wire as in a wrapped loop. Trim the excess wrapping wire.

Opening a jump ring or loop

16 Hold the jump ring or loop with chainnose and roundnose pliers or two pairs of chainnose or bentnose pliers.
17 To open the jump ring or loop, bring one pair of pliers toward you. Reverse the steps to close.

Flattened crimp

18 Hold the crimp bead with the tip of chainnose pliers. Squeeze the pliers firmly to flatten the crimp. Tug the clasp to make sure the crimp has a solid grip on the wire. If the wire slides, remove the crimp and repeat with a new crimp bead.
19 The flattened crimp.

Folded crimp

20 Position the crimp bead in the notch closest to the crimping pliers' handle.
21 Separate the wires and firmly squeeze the crimp bead.
22 Move the crimp bead into the notch at the pliers' tip. Squeeze the pliers, folding the bead in half at the indentation.
23 The folded crimp.

Overhand knot

24 Make a loop and pass the working end through it. Pull the ends to tighten the knot.

Surgeon's knot

25 Cross the right end over the left and go through the loop. Go through again. Cross the left end over the right and go through. Pull the ends to tighten the knot.

Tools & Materials

15

16

17

18

19

20

21

22

23

24

25

26

Checking the fit and finishing the necklace or bracelet

26 Check the fit of the piece against your neck or wrist, and add or remove beads if necessary. On each end, string a spacer, a crimp, a spacer, and half the clasp. Go back through the beads just strung and tighten the wire. Crimp the crimp beads and trim the excess wire.

STANDARD TOOLS

Chainnose pliers have smooth, flat inner jaws, and the tips taper to a point. Use them for gripping, and for opening and closing loops and jump rings.

Roundnose pliers have smooth, tapered, conical jaws used to make loops. The closer to the tip you work, the smaller the loop will be.

Crimping pliers have two grooves in their jaws that are used to fold or roll a crimp bead into a compact shape.

With **diagonal wire cutters**, use the front of the blades to make a pointed cut and the back of the blades to make a flat cut.

A **hammer** is used to harden and texture wire. Any hammer with a flat head will work, as long as the head is free of nicks that could mar your metal. The light ball-peen hammer shown here is one of the most commonly used hammers for jewelry making.

A **bench block** provides a hard, smooth surface on which to hammer your pieces. An anvil is similarly hard but has different surfaces, such as a tapered horn, to help form wire into different shapes.

Metal files are used to refine and shape the edges of metal and wire surfaces.

chainnose pliers

roundnose pliers

crimping pliers

diagonal wire cutters

hammer

bench block

metal files

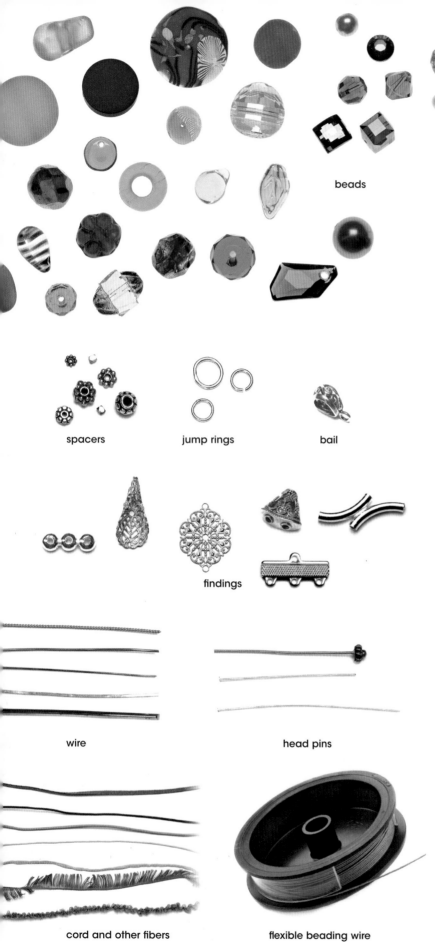

beads

spacers

jump rings

bail

findings

wire

head pins

cord and other fibers

flexible beading wire

BEADS & FINDINGS

Beads come in an incredible range of colors, shapes, and sizes, and are made from a variety of materials, including crystal and glass, gemstones, pearls and shells, metals, and wood and other natural materials.

Spacers are small beads used between larger beads to space the beads' placement.

Jump rings connect two components. They are small wire circles or ovals that are either soldered or open.

A **bail** is used to connect or position a pendant over one or more strands of a necklace.

Findings connect and position the elements of your jewelry, or may even serve as the main focal point of a piece. In multistrand jewelry, filigree components, cones, and three-to-one connectors are useful elements for connecting many strands to one strand, or many strands to a clasp.

STRINGING MATERIALS

Wire is available in a number of materials and finishes — brass, gold, gold-filled, gold-plated, fine silver, sterling silver, anodized niobium (chemically colored wire), and copper — and in varying hardnesses and shapes. Wire thickness is measured by gauge; the higher the gauge, the thinner the wire.

Memory wire is hardened steel that keep its shape after uncoiling. It is available in ring and bracelet diameters.

A **head pin** looks like a long, thick, blunt sewing pin. It has a flat or decorative head on one end to keep the beads in place. Head pins come in different diameters, or gauges, and lengths ranging from 1–3 in. (2.5–7.6cm).

Cord and other fibers are alternative stringing options; ensure that the holes in your beads are large enough for the cord to pass through, as most fibers are thicker than beading wire.

Flexible beading wire is composed of steel wires twisted together and covered with nylon.

Chain is made in many finishes (sterling silver, gold-filled, base metal, plated metal) and styles (curb, figaro, long-and-short, rolo, cable). Often chain links can be opened in the same way loops and jump rings are opened.

FINISHING MATERIALS

Crimp beads are small, large-holed, thin-walled metal beads designed to be flattened or crimped into a tight roll. A **crimp bead cover** can be closed over the crimp, mimicking the look of a small bead.

Clasps come in many sizes and shapes. Some of the most common are the toggle, consisting of a ring and a bar; lobster claw, which opens when you pull a tiny lever; S-hook, which links two rings; magnetic; hook-and-eye, consisting of a hook and a ring; slide, consisting of one tube that slides inside another; and box. Some multistrand pieces require a multistrand clasp, while other projects connect several strands to a single-strand clasp.

TOOL TIPS FROM NAOMI

Consider getting additional tools to help you construct your multistrand jewelry. The Chain Sta, with pegs for hanging chain, was a lifesaver when I made my Gem Collection Necklace (p. 42). 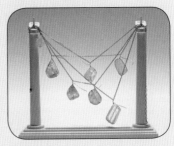 Without it, the delicate pieces of chain would have gotten tangled. Repositioning nugget units was easier when the chain was draped rather than flat. When checking the fit, I simply turned the device around and lifted the necklace off the pegs to try it on. Even if you rig your own version by hanging a project on pencils propped in mugs, it's helpful to use a tool that acts like a second set of hands.

If time is an issue, don't forget about tools that will help your efficiency. For example, a Bead Spinner will help you string individual seed bead strands faster.

Use a beading board, neck form, or anything else that helps you see your project take shape.

One tool I use with every single multistrand necklace I make: a double-sided makeup mirror. I prop it at the desired angle beforehand so when I'm in the middle of a project, I don't have to pick up a hand mirror or walk into another room to see how it looks.

crimp beads   crimp bead cover

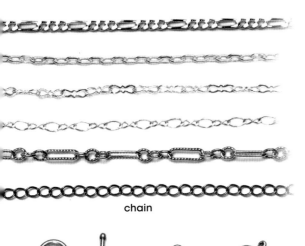

chain

clasps

Multistrand Secrets for Success

Smaller beads in the back make the fit more comfortable.

always clasp the same link to check the fit. (By the way, if you have long hair, pull it back into a ponytail first — you'll avoid getting taped strands caught in your hair.)

Minimize bulk at the ends of the necklace. If your necklace has big beads at the ends, it won't be comfortable against the back of your neck. Furthermore, the bulk may prevent the strands from laying correctly. There are many ways to avoid this. You can: Gather the strands in a cone (for an example, see the Fiesta Necklace on p. 72); string

smaller beads on the ends (Half & Half, p. 53); or use connectors or a multistrand clasp that prevent the strands from bunching (Focus on Filigree, p. 58). One other option: Instead of stringing the necklace pattern all the way to the ends, create the front part of the necklace and then attach a single strand to finish it (Chained Up, p. 36).

Make sure your clasp is large enough. There are many ways to finish necklaces and bracelets, but it's critical that the clasp can support the weight of the strands. Large lobster claw clasps and toggles are good options. If you use a box clasp, consider one with a safety catch.

In addtion to security, consider appearance. Think about how prominent you want the finish

Every project in this book contains one or more secrets for success to aid you along the way as you conceive, design, string, and finish stunning multistrand jewelry. Here's some additional hints from Naomi to help you get started!

Measure carefully. When you're working with beading wire, it's difficult to finish with a piece that's just a little too short. When possible, cut extra-long lengths of wire — just not so long that they're unmanageable. Keep in mind that, based on the drape, one strand might be 1 in. (2.5cm) longer than the previous one, while the next is 2 in. (5cm) longer. The difference between the strands will be greater as the strands get longer.

Use the largest diameter of beading wire or cord that will

fit through the beads. Typically, thicker stringing material will be more durable. If necessary, finish with large-hole beads that can accommodate a second pass of beading wire or cord.

Check the drape and fit often. If there was only one secret to multistrand success, this would be it! All the measuring in the world won't make a difference unless you try on the necklace and make adjustments frequently. The difference between a good fit and a great one may be only a few millimeters: one bead. Also, by checking the fit often, you'll be less likely to overtighten or leave gaps in the stringing material. So take the time to check the fit of each strand, the grouped strands, and the almost-finished piece before you attach the clasp. If you're attaching a chain extender,

Large clasps support the weight of heavy gemstone strands.

to be. You can finish with seed beads or large-hole spacers if you prefer a simple and streamlined look. For a professional-looking finish, you can use cones. In addition to metal, there are many options to choose from, including glass and enameled cones. Cones will draw attention to the back of the necklace and add a couple inches to the overall length — which can also be handy if you're short on beads.

Crimp and knot properly. This is especially important with multistrand pieces because the strands may pull against each other. Whether you use crimp tubes or round crimp beads, make sure your folded or flattened crimp is secure. Tug on the beading wire to make sure the crimp holds the wire firmly. If not, try again — and restring if necessary. If you need to review crimping basics, see p. 6.

If you finish with knots, make sure they're secure. Sure, it's common sense, but it's worth remembering: Most necklaces and bracelets break near the clasp attachment, not in the middle of the piece.

Be patient. Before I commit to a multistrand necklace or bracelet by attaching a clasp, I let it sit for at least a day. By approaching it with fresh eyes, I can try it on with a different top and make sure that the strands are indeed at the desired length. In addition, I can catch mistakes I've made in stringing the patterns. A couple of times when I've been in a hurry to get to the "Ta da!" moment, I've had to restring later. So pace yourself: A five-strand necklace might not be a great option to make if you're looking for something to wear in the next hour.

MORE TIPS FROM NAOMI!

Here are a few tips that are perennial favorites for beading projects with one to 100 strands. These optional ideas will help you get great results, but you won't need to use them in every project.

• Use crimp covers to fill gaps in beading wire. If you discover a gap in your stringing material after you've finished the piece, crimp covers can save the day. Either attach them near the finishing or use them as a design element by attaching them throughout the strands.

• If the bead holes are large enough, loop the beading wire back through the beads on the end of each strand. This is a way to temporarily secure the beads without using tape (which can get unwieldy when you're checking the fit often). Also, tape can accidentally fall off. Beads that are temporarily knotted are more likely to pull downward, thus making the knot more secure rather than loosening it.

• Use a bead reamer to smooth out rough spots inside beads. Burrs can abrade the stringing material and cause it to break. While it might not be practical to check every bead, consider it a good habit to get into.

• Save your extra beads and make a quick project — right away! After I finished the Mint Medley necklace (p. 16), I had a few jade rounds left. I could have made a bracelet or earrings, but I wasn't in the mood for a matched set. So I whipped up a single-strand necklace and finished with black faceted beads. After the challenge of designing and completing the three-strand necklace, the single strand was a welcome break.

Cones will draw attention to the back of the necklace and add length.

Projects

Multicolored Multifaceted Multistrand

by Naomi Fujimoto

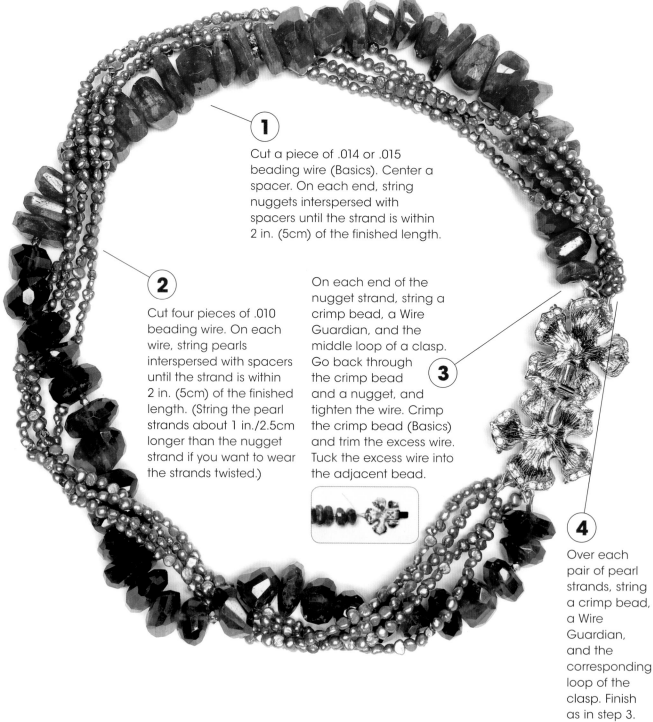

1 Cut a piece of .014 or .015 beading wire (Basics). Center a spacer. On each end, string nuggets interspersed with spacers until the strand is within 2 in. (5cm) of the finished length.

2 Cut four pieces of .010 beading wire. On each wire, string pearls interspersed with spacers until the strand is within 2 in. (5cm) of the finished length. (String the pearl strands about 1 in./2.5cm longer than the nugget strand if you want to wear the strands twisted.)

3 On each end of the nugget strand, string a crimp bead, a Wire Guardian, and the middle loop of a clasp. Go back through the crimp bead and a nugget, and tighten the wire. Crimp the crimp bead (Basics) and trim the excess wire. Tuck the excess wire into the adjacent bead.

4 Over each pair of pearl strands, string a crimp bead, a Wire Guardian, and the corresponding loop of the clasp. Finish as in step 3.

Pair the best and brightest in gemstones: Faceted rubies and amethysts make a striking color-blocked necklace. Adding tiny pearls and vermeil spacers unifies the design. The visual weight of the four pearl strands together equals the weight of the gemstone strand.

Secret for Success

Many pieces with multiple strands look best when the strands are slightly twisted before the jewelry is worn. Twist gently, and don't twist the clasp; that puts extra stress on the finishing and can cause breakage.

TECHNIQUES

Five strands
- using a multistrand clasp
- using a clasp as a focal

SUPPLIES

18½ in. (47cm)
- **2** 8-in. (20cm) strands 11–14mm faceted gemstone nuggets
- **4–5** 16-in. (41cm) strands 3mm pearls
- **35–50** 3mm spacers

- flexible beading wire, .010
- flexible beading wire, .014 or .015
- **6** crimp beads
- **6** Wire Guardians
- three-strand box clasp
- chainnose or crimping pliers
- diagonal wire cutters

Design alternative

Few looks can beat the impact of a lush multistrand gemstone necklace. This variation by Linda Augsburg features the same experimentation with texture and facets that Naomi's necklace boasts, but achieves it by using five different sizes and shapes of the same gemstone, howlite. (Even the red rounds are dyed howlite.)

Mint medley

by Naomi Fujimoto

1 To make the pendant, cut a 6-in. (15cm) piece of 24-gauge wire. Center a coin bead on the wire. Twist the wire halves together next to the bead.

2 Over both ends of the wire, string three or four flowers, from smallest to largest, and a spacer. Make a wrapped loop (Basics).

3 For the shortest strand, cut a 20–22-in. (51–56cm) piece of beading wire. Stringing an 8º seed bead after each bead, string: 20mm round bead, coin, 16mm round bead, coin, 14mm round bead, coin. Repeat until the strand is within 2 in. (5cm) of the finished length.

The strands in this necklace have essentially the same pattern; start each with a different bead in the sequence to emphasize the necklace's asymmetry. When you check the fit of this necklace, you won't necessarily add or remove equal numbers of beads from each end. Instead, adjust each strand while keeping the overall balance of the necklace in mind.

Secret for Success

When finishing, it's not necessary to string the same number of 6mm beads on each end. Use them to make minor adjustments in the length of each strand. Also, if a strand ends with a larger bead, string two or three 6mms instead for a less bulky finish.

TECHNIQUES

Three strands
- using a single-strand clasp
- using a focal bead on one strand only

SUPPLIES

16–19 in. (38–51cm)
- **3–4** 40–80mm metal flowers with center holes
- 16-in. (41cm) strand 20mm round faceted beads
- 16-in. (41cm) strand 16mm round beads
- **13–17** 14mm round faceted beads
- 16-in. (41cm) strand 10mm coin beads
- **12–24** 6mm round faceted beads
- 3g 8º hex-cut seed beads
- 4–5mm flat spacer
- flexible beading wire, .018 or .019
- 6 in. (15cm) 24-gauge wire
- 1½-in. (3.8cm) head pin
- **6** crimp beads
- **6** crimp covers
- 25–30mm lobster claw clasp
- 1½-in. (3.8cm) chain for extender, 12–15mm links
- chainnose and roundnose pliers
- diagonal wire cutters
- crimping pliers (optional)

4

5

6

7

4 For the middle strand, cut a 23–26-in. (58–66cm) piece of beading wire. Starting with a 16mm, repeat the pattern from step 3 until the strand is about two-thirds the finished length. String five to seven 8ºs, the pendant, and five to seven 8ºs. Continue stringing the beaded pattern until the strand is within 2 in. (5cm) of the finished length.

5 For the longest strand, cut a 25–30-in. (64–76cm) piece of beading wire. Starting with a

14mm, repeat the pattern from step 3 until the strand is within 2 in. (5cm) of the finished length.

6 On one side, on each end, string one to three 6mm round beads, a crimp bead, and a 6mm round. Over all three wires, string a lobster claw clasp. Repeat on the other side, substituting a 1½-in. (3.8cm) piece of chain for the clasp. Check the fit, and add or remove beads if necessary. Go back through the last few beads strung and tighten the wires.

Crimp the crimp beads (Basics) and trim the excess wire. Attach crimp covers over each crimp.

7 On a head pin, string a bead. Make the first half of a wrapped loop. Attach the end link of chain and complete the wraps.

Crystal Rhythms

by Linda Hartung

Music-lover Linda enjoys incorporating beat, tempo, and rhythm into a piece of jewelry, and envisioned the three strands of this necklace, each with a distinct pattern, as bars of music. She connected the bars using double-holed keystone crystals to create a "polyrhythm" — the simultaneous sound of two or more independent rhythms — and changed the number and size of the crystals in each strand to create different tempos. The result is a fabulous, undulating score of crystals that drapes beautifully in three distinct but harmonious design tempos.

TECHNIQUES

Three strands
- using a multistrand clasp
- making connections between the strands

SUPPLIES

16½ in. (41.9cm)
- **6** 17mm keystone crystals
- **6** 13mm keystone crystals

- **14** 10mm round pearls
- **10** 8mm round pearls
- **6** 6mm round pearls
- **57** 4mm round pearls
- **28** 6mm top-drilled bicone crystals
- **77** 4.5mm simplicity crystals
- **51** 4mm bicone or Xilion crystals
- 1g 14º seed beads
- flexible beading wire, .018 or .019
- **6** crimp beads

- **6** bell end-caps
- three-strand flamenco clasp
- chainnose and roundnose pliers, or **2** pairs of chainnose pliers
- diagonal wire cutters
- crimping pliers (optional)
- two-part epoxy

TIPS

The challenge of this necklace is creating three different patterns that will synchronize and finish at the precise measure. Therefore, it's important to note:
- Even though 14º seed beads were used in both necklaces shown here, there was a very slight difference in the size of the gold and silver beads. Where eight seed beads were used for the segments of the gold necklace, seven were used in the silver version. In larger quantities, the small size differences in the beads worked themselves out, so in the 10- and 11-bead special segments, no adjustments were made.

- Of the 57 4mm pearls, 29 are in one color for the outer strand, and 28 are in a second color for the middle strand.
- Of the 77 4.5mm simplicity crystals, 57 are in one color and 20 are in a second color. In the gold necklace, the second color is only used in the inner strand. In the silver necklace, the two colors are intermingled in the inner and outer strands.
- Xilion beads from Create Your Style with Swarovski Elements can be used in place of the bicones without any adjustments to bead count or measurements necessary. Strand a uses 4mm bicones; strand b uses 4mm Xilions.

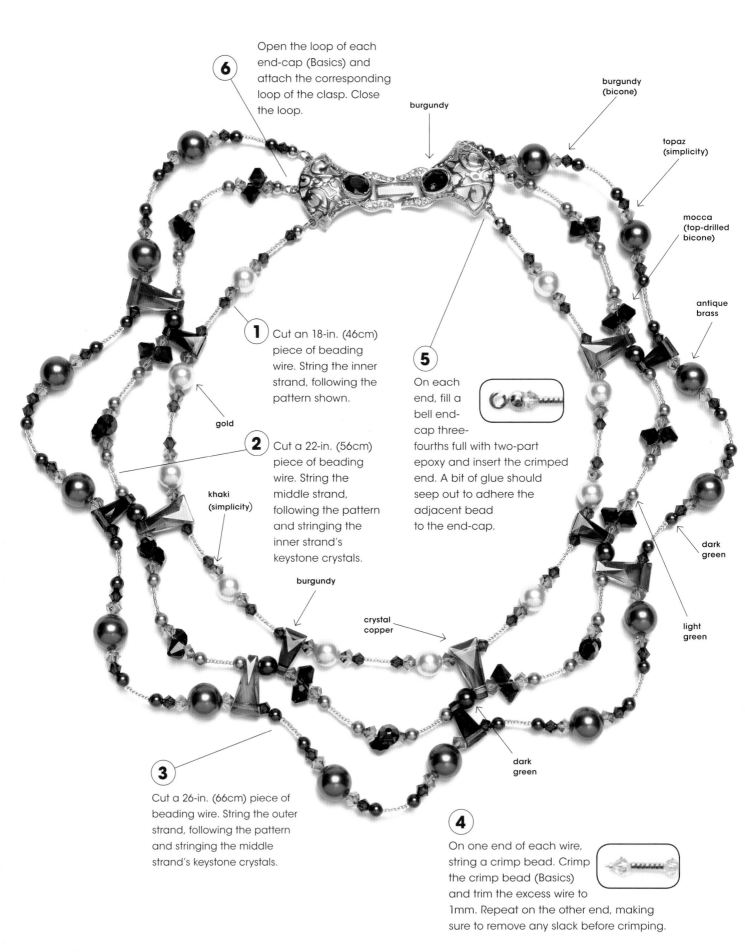

6 Open the loop of each end-cap (Basics) and attach the corresponding loop of the clasp. Close the loop.

burgundy

burgundy (bicone)

topaz (simplicity)

mocca (top-drilled bicone)

antique brass

1 Cut an 18-in. (46cm) piece of beading wire. String the inner strand, following the pattern shown.

gold

5 On each end, fill a bell end-cap three-fourths full with two-part epoxy and insert the crimped end. A bit of glue should seep out to adhere the adjacent bead to the end-cap.

2 Cut a 22-in. (56cm) piece of beading wire. String the middle strand, following the pattern and stringing the inner strand's keystone crystals.

khaki (simplicity)

dark green

burgundy

light green

crystal copper

3 Cut a 26-in. (66cm) piece of beading wire. String the outer strand, following the pattern and stringing the middle strand's keystone crystals.

dark green

4 On one end of each wire, string a crimp bead. Crimp the crimp bead (Basics) and trim the excess wire to 1mm. Repeat on the other end, making sure to remove any slack before crimping.

Bead Showcase

by Jane Konkel

Display your favorite beads on one strand of a three-strand bracelet—choose a theme for your charms, or mix and match them for an eclectic effect. Because this is a looped single strand, it can also do double duty as a casual necklace.

TECHNIQUES

Three strands

- looping a single strand for a multistrand effect
- adding dangles

SUPPLIES

8 in. (20cm)

- 28mm fish pendant
- 18–22mm cinnabar bead
- 18mm heart pendant
- 16mm bone bead
- **2–4** 3mm spacers
- **2–4** 5mm bead caps
- 19½–24 in. (49.5–61cm) 3mm ball chain
- **2** 2-in. (5cm) head pins
- **4** 10mm jump rings
- **2** 10mm split rings
- **2** ball chain end-ring connectors
- lobster claw clasp
- chainnose pliers
- diagonal wire cutters
- roundnose pliers
- split-ring pliers (optional)

Secret for Success

This bracelet boasts one of the easiest multistrand effects to achieve. The technique is simple: Just coil the single long strand around your wrist several times before fastening the clasp.

1 On a head pin, string a bead cap or spacer, the bone bead, and a bead cap. Make a wrapped loop (Basics), completing the wraps. Repeat with the cinnabar bead.

2 Cut a piece of chain three times the circumference of your wrist. On each end, attach an end-ring connector and a split ring. On one end, attach a lobster claw clasp.

3 Open a 10mm jump ring (Basics). Attach a heart pendant and the chain. Close the jump ring. Repeat with the fish pendant and the bead units.

Seeds
of
Change

by Karli Sullivan

Versatility is the name of the game in this necklace: Change the number of seed bead strands you use for a denser or lighter drape. Add or subtract strands to create a new color scheme. Swap out one pendant for another. With so many options for customizing and re-customizing your necklace, this truly is a piece that can go with any outfit!

Secret for Success

A combination of magnetic and lobster claw clasps and of a rainbow of interchangeable seed bead strands means this project offers endless possibilities. After all, how many multistrand pieces can boast three strands one day — and six the next?

TECHNIQUES
Four-Six strands
- centering a pendant over all strands
- creating a necklace with an adjustable strand count
- making your own bail

SUPPLIES
19 in. (48cm)
- pendant(s) with large hole or bail to accommodate seed bead strands
- 2g 11° or 4g 8° seed beads per strand
- flexible beading wire, .014 or .015

- **2** 5mm inside diameter (ID) soldered jump rings per strand
- **2** 4mm ID jump rings
- **2** crimp beads per strand
- magnetic clasp
- **2** lobster claw clasps
- chainnose or crimping pliers
- diagonal wire cutters

1 Cut a piece of beading wire (Basics). String a crimp bead and a soldered jump ring. Go back through the crimp bead and tighten the wire. Crimp the crimp bead (Basics).

2 String seed beads, covering the wire tail, until the strand is within 1 in. (2.5cm) of the desired length.

3 String a crimp bead and a soldered jump ring. Go back through the last few beads strung and tighten the wire. Check the fit, and add or remove beads if necessary. Crimp the crimp bead and trim the excess wire. Repeat steps 1–3 for each strand.

4 Use a jump ring to attach a lobster claw clasp to each half of a magnetic clasp.

5 To make a bail, string seed beads, a pendant, and a crimp bead on a 6-in. (15cm) piece of beading wire. Go through the crimp bead and several adjacent beads with the wire end. Tighten the wire. Crimp the crimp bead and trim the excess wire. Center the pendant over the desired number of strands. Attach each end of each strand to one of the lobster claw clasps.

TIP
Incorporate small beads or crystals in each strand to add texture and sparkle.

Design Alternatives

Adjust the color combinations, number of strands, pendants, bails — the choices are all yours as you make your own Seeds of Change design.

Elegant Eight

by Michelle Gowland

Talk about lush! Eight
strands of pearls and
chains give this bracelet
texture, movement, and
dimension.

TECHNIQUES

Eight strands

- using a multistrand clasp
- adding dangles

SUPPLIES

7½ in. (19.1cm)

- **20–25** 13–15mm (large) pearls in mixed shapes and colors
- **35–45** 8–10mm (medium) pearls in mixed shapes and colors
- **70–110** 4–5mm (small) crystals and pearls in mixed shapes and colors
- 60–74 in. (1.5–1.9m) 22-gauge wire
- 7–7½ in. (18–19.1cm) chain, 20–30mm (large) links
- 21–23 in. (53–58cm) chain, 4–7mm (small) links
- **38** 1½-in. (3.8cm) head pins
- **65–73** 4–5mm jump rings
- four-strand slide clasp
- chainnose pliers
- diagonal wire cutters
- roundnose pliers

Secret for Success

Before attaching the second end of each strand, close the clasp. This makes it easier to attach corresponding clasp loops and ensures that you don't overtighten the wires before crimping.

1

3

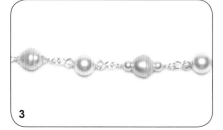

2

4

5

6

7

1 Cut a 2-in. (5cm) piece of wire and make a plain loop (Basics). String one to three beads, including one large or medium pearl. Make a plain loop. Make a total of 18 to 22 large- and medium-pearl units.

2 Open a jump ring (Basics) and attach two pearl units. Close the jump ring. Continue attaching units until you've made a 7–7½-in.

(18–19.1cm) strand. Make a second strand with the remaining units.

3 Cut a 1½-in. (3.8cm) piece of wire and make a plain loop. String a small crystal or pearl, a medium pearl, and a small crystal or pearl. Make a plain loop. Make 16 to 20 medium-pearl units. Repeat step 2.

4 On a head pin, string one to three beads, including one medium or large pearl. Make a wrapped loop (Basics). Make a total of 15 medium- and large-pearl dangles. On a head pin, string a small crystal or pearl. Make a wrapped loop. Make 15 small-bead dangles.

5 Cut three 7–7½-in. (18–19.1cm) pieces of small-link chain. Use a jump ring to attach two dangles from step 4 and a link of chain. Attach five pairs of dangles to each chain.

6 Repeat step 4 to make a total of four medium- and large-pearl dangles and four small-bead dangles. Cut a 7–7½-in. (18–19.1cm) piece of large-link chain. Use jump rings to attach four pairs of dangles to the chain.

7 Arrange the strands and chains on your work surface. Working in pairs of strands and/or chains, use a jump ring to attach each end of each strand to a loop of a slide clasp.

Design Alternatives

For a similar look without wrapped loops, try simply stringing your beads on flexible beading wire and attaching to the multistrand clasp with crimps. Karin Van Voorhees's five-strand bracelet showcases three different sizes of lapis lazuli rounds, while Naomi Fujimoto's three-strand collects a variety of sizes and shapes of glass beads around an earthy green-and-brown palette.

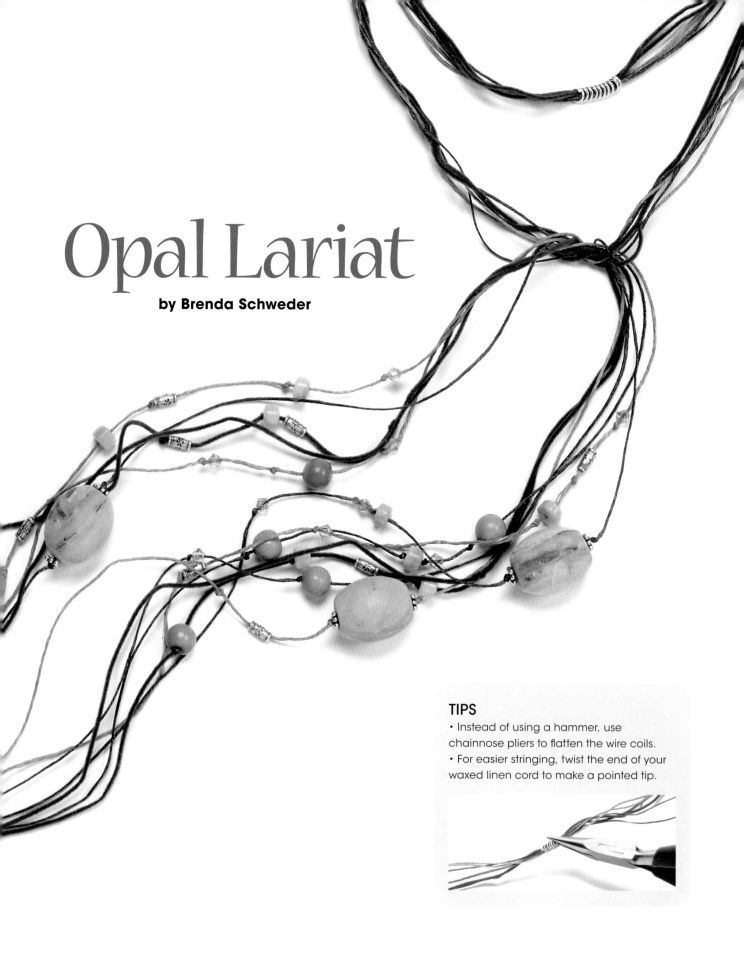

Opal Lariat
by Brenda Schweder

TIPS
• Instead of using a hammer, use chainnose pliers to flatten the wire coils.
• For easier stringing, twist the end of your waxed linen cord to make a pointed tip.

Multiple strands of linen and velvet add to the dimension of this design. A lariat-style necklace can be worn a variety of ways: Loosely tie the ends, as shown, double the wrap around your neck before tying, or consider looping the necklace in half and passing the ends through.

Secrets for Success

Many multistrand pieces are prone to tangling when they're not being worn. Try storing your lariat on a wire hanger so it doesn't get tangled.

To ensure random beads fall where you want them, try draping a "rough draft" over a dress form or a model before permanently placing them.

TECHNIQUES

Six strands

- creating front closure/lariat style
- making your own closure
- knotting

SUPPLIES

5 ft. (1.5m)

- **3** 20mm opal beads
- **6–10** 8mm round beads
- **8–12** 6–7mm rondelles
- **8–12** 6mm silver tube beads
- **7–10** 4mm bicone crystals
- **6** 4mm flat spacers
- 20 ft. (6.1m) 4-ply waxed linen, in slate grey and charcoal
- 10 ft. (3m) Petite Very Velvet nylon cord
- 23 in. (58cm) 22-gauge half-hard wire
- diagonal wire cutters
- bench block or anvil
- drill bit or knitting needle with a 2–3mm diameter
- hammer

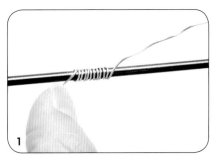

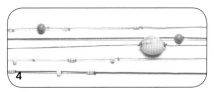

1 Cut a 23-in. (58cm) piece of wire. Holding one end down, wrap the wire tightly around a drill bit or knitting needle. After you've made a coil almost 2 in. (5cm) long, remove the coil. Cut the coil into five small coils.

2 Cut two 5-ft. (1.5m) pieces of the following: slate grey waxed linen, charcoal waxed linen, Petite Very Velvet. Center a coil over all six pieces. On a bench block or anvil, hammer the coil. On each

side, over all the strands, string a coil 4½ in. (11.4cm) from the previous one. Hammer the coil. Repeat.

3 On one waxed linen strand, about 10 in. (25cm) from the end, tie an overhand knot (Basics). String a spacer, a 20mm opal bead, and a spacer. Tie an overhand knot. String a rondelle and tie a knot 1½ in. (3.8cm) from the previous bead. String a bicone crystal and tie a knot.

String another bicone and tie a knot about 1 in. (2.5cm) away.

4 Starting 9–11 in. (23–28cm) from the other end of the strand, string beads and tie knots as desired. Starting 9–11 in. (23–28cm) from the end of each remaining strand, string beads and tie knots as desired, staggering the placement of beads on each strand. Trim the strands if desired.

Brass and Blue

by Helene Tsigistras

Brass paired with turquoise blue is a beautiful combination. The pendant is the focal point of this stunning piece: Enameled and coated with antitarnish lacquer, it was made in a South African village by local craftspeople employed by Metalcraft by DeZine. The large holes in each corner make it perfect for a multistrand attachment.

TECHNIQUES

Three strands

- finishing with cones
- attaching strands to either side of a focal

SUPPLIES

21 in. (53cm)

- 50mm pendant, with two holes
- 16-in. (41cm) strand 13mm tube beads
- 16-in. (41cm) strand 12mm lava rock coins
- 16-in. (41cm) strand 5mm round beads
- **2** 6mm spacers
- flexible beading wire, .014 or .015
- **2** cones
- **4** crimp beads
- **2** hook clasps
- chainnose or crimping pliers
- diagonal wire cutters

TIP

If you like the look of a twisted necklace, loosely braid the strands before stringing the cones.

1 Cut three pieces of beading wire (Basics). Cut the wires in half. Over three wires, string a crimp bead and a hole of the pendant. Go back through the crimp bead and tighten the wires. Crimp the crimp bead (Basics). Repeat on the other side of the pendant.

2 On each side, over two wires, string a tube bead. Separate the wires. On one wire, string coins; on the other, string tubes until the strands are within 2 in. (5cm) of the finished length.

3 On each of the remaining wires, string 5mm rounds until the strands are within 2 in. (5cm) of the finished length.

4 On each side, over all three wires, string a cone, a 6mm spacer, a crimp bead, and a clasp. Check the fit, and add or remove beads if necessary. Go back through the crimp bead and tighten the wires. Crimp the crimp bead and trim the excess wire.

by Addie Kidd

Carnelian Cascade

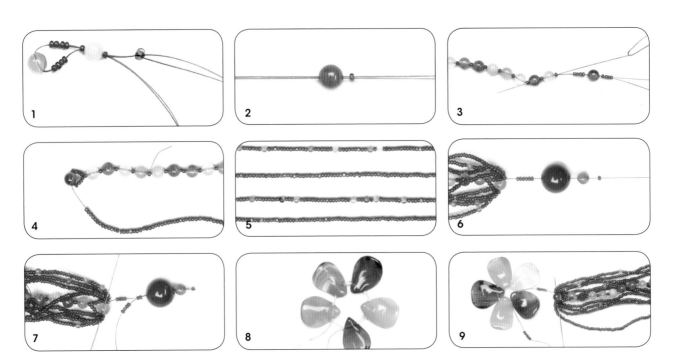

Combine beauty with practicality in this piece when you use ribbon elastic and petal-shaped beads to make a pretty clasp for your necklace. In this twist on a button-and-loop closure, the round carnelian beads push through the open gemstone flower at the front to secure the lush strands.

TECHNIQUES

Eight–12 strands

- creating your own clasp
- using many similar and one different strands

SUPPLIES

16 in. (41cm)

- **5** 15mm petal-shaped carnelian beads
- 10mm round carnelian bead
- 16-in. (41cm) strand 6mm round carnelian beads
- **1–2** 16-in. (41cm) strands 2mm round carnelian beads
- **2** hanks 13º Charlottes, deep red
- 12 in. (30cm) ribbon elastic
- K.O. beading thread, red
- G-S Hypo Cement
- beading needles, #13
- Big Eye needle

1 Center a beading needle on 2 yd. (1.8m) of thread. Using it doubled, pick up a stop bead, leaving a 6-in. (15cm) tail. Pick up a Charlotte, a 6mm round, five Charlottes, a 6mm, and four Charlottes. Skip the last nine beads and go back through the first three beads picked up to form a loop. Pull the loop snug.

2 Pick up a 6mm and a Charlotte. Repeat until the necklace is within 2 in. (5cm) of the finished length. End with a Charlotte. Reserve a 6mm for the clasp.

3 Pick up four Charlottes, a 6mm, and four Charlottes. Skip these nine beads and go back through the last few beads added. Tighten the thread. End the thread and tails by going back through a few beads and tying half-hitch knots between them as you go. Dot the knots with glue.

4 Thread a needle on the end of 2 yd. (1.8m) of thread. Go through the last 2 in. (5cm) of the necklace, leaving a 1-in. (2.5cm) tail. Tie half-hitch knots between beads, and exit the end 6mm. Pick up enough Charlottes to equal the length of the necklace, plus a few extra to create slack. Go through the last 6mm at the opposite end of the necklace. Check that the strand is a pleasing length, and adjust if necessary.

5 Pick up Charlottes as in step 4 and go through the 6mm at the beginning of the necklace. Continue and make seven to 11 more strands — some with Charlottes and some with Charlottes interspersed with 2mm beads. Add thread as needed. Stop when the holes of the end 6mms are nearly full. End the threads as in step 3.

6 Thread a needle on the end of 2 yd. (1.8m) of thread. Secure the thread at one end of the necklace by tying half-hitch knots, as in step 4. Exit the end 6mm. Pick up six Charlottes, a 10mm carnelian bead, a 6mm, and a Charlotte.

7 Skip the last Charlotte, and sew back through the 6mm, 10mm, and two Charlottes. Pick up four Charlottes, sew through the other side of the end 6mm, and pull tight. Retrace the thread path and end the thread as in step 3. Dot the knots with glue.

8 Thread a Big Eye needle on the ribbon elastic, and pick up five petal beads, making sure that they face in the same direction. Go through all five beads again, and pull the elastic snug. Make a surgeon's knot (Basics) and pull the ends tight. Dot the knot with glue, and trim the excess elastic.

9 Secure 2 yd. (1.8m) of thread at the end of the necklace and exiting the 6mm. Pick up five Charlottes, and go through one petal bead of the flower. Pick up five Charlottes, and go through the other side of the 6mm. Make sure that the Charlottes create a loop on the underside of the petal, and pull the loop tight. Retrace the thread path, and end the thread with half-hitch knots between beads. Dot the knots with glue.

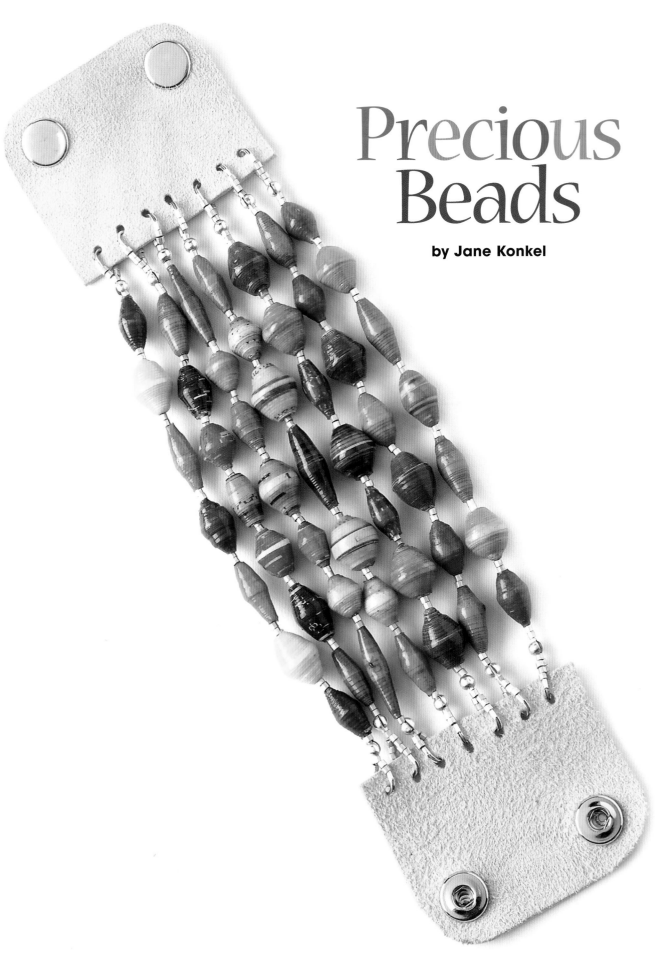

Precious Beads

by Jane Konkel

A pre-made leather end component like this is an easy way to approach a multistrand bracelet. You're guaranteed even placement and a secure fit. Take care to balance colors and shapes as you work, as noted in the instructions. These cheerfully colored beads are the product of BeadforLife (beadforlife.org), a nonprofit organization that creates jobs for a group of Ugandan people fleeing war or living with HIV/AIDS.

Secret for Success

Multistrand pieces invite options and experimentation with their many layers. In this bracelet, for example, you can string a multitude of colors on each strand. Or, for a more uniform look, arrange beads in one shade on each strand, as pictured below.

TECHNIQUES

Seven strands
- attaching individual strands to leather bracelet ends
- crimping

SUPPLIES

7–8 in. (18–20cm)
- 2-oz. (57g) bag 10–26mm mixed paper beads (approximately 170 beads)
- 2g 11° cylinder beads
- flexible beading wire, .013 or .014
- 50 x 60mm seven-hole leather end component
- **14** crimp beads
- **14** crimp covers
- **14** Wire Guardians
- chainnose pliers
- diagonal wire cutters
- crimping pliers (optional)

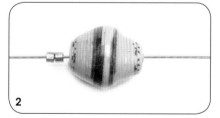

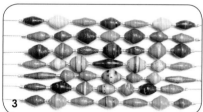

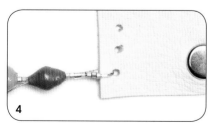

1 Decide how long you want your bracelet to be, add 3 in. (7.6cm), and cut seven pieces of beading wire to that length. Center a paper bead on one wire.

2 On each end, string two cylinder beads and a paper bead. Repeat until the beaded section is within 3 in. (7.6cm) of the finished length, ending with cylinder beads.

3 String the pattern in steps 1 and 2 on the remaining wires, balancing different colors and shapes.

4 On each end of one wire, string a crimp bead, three to five cylinder beads, a Wire Guardian, and the corresponding hole of a leather end component. Check the fit, and add or remove beads from each end if necessary. String two to four cylinder beads and go back through one cylinder bead, the crimp bead, and a few more beads. Crimp the crimp bead (Basics) and trim the excess wire. Use chainnose pliers to close a crimp cover over the crimp bead. Repeat with the remaining wires.

Chained Up

by Naomi Fujimoto

1

2

3

1 On a bench block or anvil, gently hammer three 14–18mm jump rings. If they open, use two pairs of pliers to close them (Basics).

2 Cut a 17–21-in. (43–53cm) piece of beading wire. String a 22–25mm bead and a bicone crystal. Repeat until the strand is 10–14 in. (25–36cm), ending with a large bead. (The ends of each strand should just reach the sides of your neck.) On each end, string a crimp bead and a Wire Guardian. Go back through the crimp bead and an adjacent bead. Tighten the wire and crimp the crimp bead (Basics).

3 Open two hammered jump rings. Attach each end of the beaded strand. Cut a chain to the desired length and attach each end link to a jump ring. Continue cutting chains and attaching them to the jump rings as you go, checking the drape of each. (My chains are 10–13 in./ 25–33cm; each is about 1 in./2.5cm longer than the previous one.) Close each jump ring.

Give chain remnants new life in a perfectly draped collar. You'll need only a foot or so of each kind, plus a few inches for finishing. And remember that "mixed metals" doesn't have to be all-inclusive: Naomi used silver, gunmetal, and brass for a cool palette.

Secret for Success

Save your expensive chain for another project; here, the pieces serve primarily as a multistrand backdrop for the puffy metallic beads.

TECHNIQUES

Six strands
- making a single-strand back, multistrand front
- using many similar and one different strands

SUPPLIES

18½ in. (47cm)
- **11–14** 22–25mm beads
- 14–16mm accent bead
- **11–14** 3mm bicone crystals

- flexible beading wire, .014 or .015
- 13–17 in. (33–43cm) chain, 20–25mm links
- 21–26 in. (53–66cm) chain, 16–20mm links
- 11–15 in. (28–38cm) chain, 15–18mm links
- 12–16 in. (30–41cm) chain, 10–12mm links
- 10–14 in. (25–36cm) chain, 8–10mm links
- 2-in. (5cm) head pin

- **3** 14–18mm jump rings
- **2** 6–8mm jump rings
- **2** crimp beads
- **2** Wire Guardians
- large lobster claw clasp
- bench block or anvil
- chainnose pliers
- diagonal wire cutters
- hammer
- roundnose pliers
- crimping pliers (optional)
- heavy-duty wire cutters (optional)

TIP

Rather than cut large-link chain, use two pairs of pliers to open and close links at the desired length. You'll prevent damaging your wire cutters and save many inches of chain in the long run.

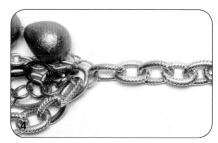

4 Cut two 3–4-in. (7.6–10cm) pieces of 16–20mm link chain. Open an end link of each as you would a jump ring, and attach the hammered jump ring on each end of the draped chains. Close the links.

5 Check the fit, and trim chain if necessary. On one end, use a pair of 6–8mm jump rings to attach an end link and a lobster claw clasp. On the other end, use a hammered jump ring to attach an end link and a 2-in. (5cm) piece of 16–20mm link chain.

6 On a head pin, string an accent bead and a bicone. Make the first half of a wrapped loop (Basics). Attach the end link and complete the wraps.

Extend a Strand

by Jane Konkel

TECHNIQUES

Three strands

- looping a single strand for a multistrand effect

SUPPLIES

57 in. (1.4m)

- **22–30** 10mm pearls
- **66–80** 8mm pearls
- **84–101** 6mm pearls
- **60–74** 4mm pearls

- flexible beading wire, .014 or .015
- **2** crimp beads
- magnetic clasp
- chainnose pliers
- crimping pliers
- diagonal wire cutters

Cultura pearls are glass beads dipped multiple times in a coating that rival the look of real pearls. These Czech glass pearls resemble more expensive glass pearls in their consistent color and uniform size, yet are considerably less costly. The design is simple — two repeated patterns using beads in four sizes. The magnetic clasp easily allows you to wrap the long strand several times around your neck, for an inexpensive and easy-to-make alternative to the classic three-strand necklace.

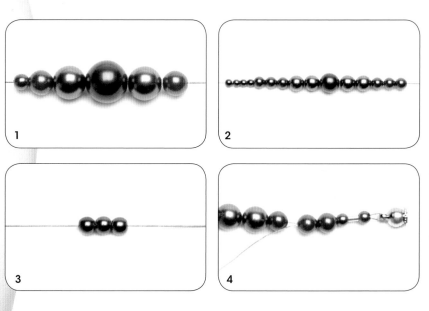

1

2

3

4

1 Cut a 1½-yd. (1.4m) piece of beading wire (Basics). String: 4mm pearl, 6mm pearl, 8mm pearl, 10mm pearl, 8mm, 6mm. Repeat the pattern three times.

2 String: four 4mms, three 6mms, two 8mms, 10mm, two 8mms, three 6mms. Repeat the pattern three times.

3 String three 4mms. String the pattern in step 1 five times. String the pattern in step 2 three times. String three 4mms. String the pattern in step 1 six times. String the pattern in step 2 twice.

4 On each end, string a 4mm, a crimp bead, a 4mm, and a clasp half. Check the fit. Add or remove beads from each end if necessary. Go back through the last beads strung and tighten the wire. Crimp the crimp bead (Basics) and trim the excess wire.

Design Alternative

The Mardi Gras-inspired colors of the necklace on p. 38 are dark olive, metallic violet, dark amethyst, and dark navy blue. For a subdued alternative, use Swarovski pearls in greys and pinks and sterling silver bead caps.

Blue Ribbon Style

by Ute Bernsen

Go with the flow of silk ribbons, balancing symmetry with casually placed knots to create richly colored waves accented by the sparkle of dichroic-glass beads. Weave the ribbons through the beads singly or together to create connections between the layers of your necklace.

Secret for Success

There are a handful of options for finishing a multistrand necklace with a single-strand clasp: crimp all the ends together, gather them through a cone, secure in a pinch end, or simply pull them through the clasp end as Ute has done here. The thicker nature of fiber strands means they fill more space, so a clasp with large loops is necessary.

TECHNIQUES

Five strands

- making connections between strands
- joining many strands on a single-strand clasp
- knotting

SUPPLIES

24 in. (61cm)

- **30–32** 8–15mm large-hole beads
- 5-ribbon silk ribbon mix
- hook clasp with large loops

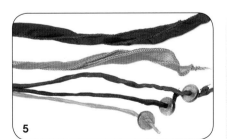

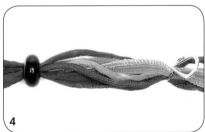

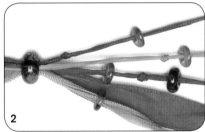

BEAD ARTIST NOTES

dichroic-glass beads by Paula Radke (paularadke.com)

borosilicate glass beads by Jenny E. from Jah-Love's Creations (jahluv420@earthlink.net, seemyglass.com)

1 Center a large bead over all five ribbons.

2 On each side, tie overhand knots (Basics) on three to five ribbons. String five small beads as shown.

3 On each end, string a large bead over all five ribbons approximately 4 in. (10cm) from the center bead. Repeat step 2.

4 On each end, over all five ribbons, string a large bead 7 in. (18cm) from the last bead strung. Decide how long you want your necklace to be. On each end, over all five ribbons, string half of a clasp, positioning it to create the desired length.

5 On each end, string a small bead on the three thinnest strands. Tie an overhand knot next to each bead.

Gem Collection Necklace

by Naomi Fujimoto

Show off a gallery of beads against a backdrop of chain in a project that's perfect for a handful of leftover nuggets or a short strand that you want to turn into a necklace. Make hammered wire frames for each bead; once you attach them, they'll pull the chain into a dramatic web. By hanging the bib on a Chain Sta while you work, you'll be able to see how the bib will drape; you can also use T-pins and a foam board.

Secret for Success

Usually you'd attach the clasp in the last step. However, in this case it's easier to check the drape of your strands by clasping and unclasping the necklace — otherwise you'll risk tangling the centerpiece.

TECHNIQUES

Four strand
- combining a single-strand back with a multistrand front
- using a Chain Sta Stabilization Solution

SUPPLIES

14–16 in. (36–41cm)
- **7–9** 18–30mm nuggets
- 6mm crystal
- 4–5 ft. (1.2–1.5m) chain, 2–3mm links
- 56–72 in. (1.4–1.8m) 24-gauge wire
- 35–45 in. (89–114cm) 26-gauge wire
- 1½-in. (3.8cm) head pin
- **2** 7–8mm jump rings
- **2** 3–4mm jump rings

- lobster claw clasp
- 2-in. (5cm) chain for extender, 4–5mm links
- bench block or anvil
- Chain Sta Stabilization Solution or foam board with T-pins
- chainnose pliers
- diagonal wire cutters
- hammer
- roundnose pliers

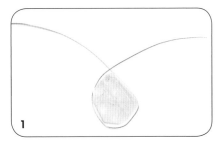

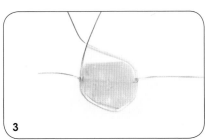

1 Cut an 8-in. (20cm) piece of 24-gauge wire. Wrap it around the perimeter of a nugget. Use your fingers to shape the wire to the nugget. Cross the wire ends above the nugget.

2 On a bench block or anvil, gently hammer the wire frame. Do not hammer the wire ends.

3 Cut a 5-in. (13cm) piece of 26-gauge wire. Center the nugget on the wire. Wrap each end of the 26-gauge wire around the frame three or four times. Trim the excess 26-gauge wire. Use chainnose pliers to tuck the wire ends against the frame.

TIPS

- When selecting chain, opt for delicate yet sturdy links. Also, make sure the hammered jump rings will fit through the end links.
- If you're working with 24-gauge wire from a spool, don't pre-cut the wire pieces in step 1. Instead, for each frame, wrap the wire around the nugget, leaving 1½ in. (3.8cm) of excess on each end. Then cut the wire. You can also use less than 5 in. (13cm) of 26-gauge wire per nugget; just make sure you have enough to make secure wraps when attaching the bead to the frame.

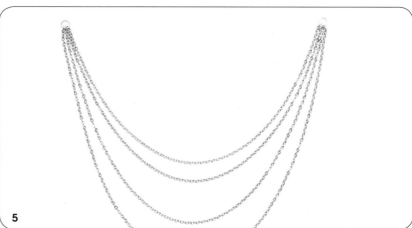

4

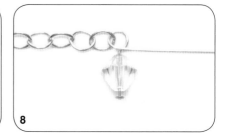

5

6

7

8

4 With one end of the 24-gauge
wire, make a set of wraps
(Basics) above the nugget. Trim the
excess wrapping wire. Make the first
half of a wrapped loop (Basics)
perpendicular to the nugget. Make
seven to nine nugget units.

5 Cut an 8–9-in., 9–10-in.,
10½–12-in., and 12–14-in.
(20–23cm, 23–25cm, 26.7–30cm,
and 30–36cm) piece of 2–3mm link
chain. Hammer two 7–8mm jump
rings. On each side, open a jump
ring (Basics) and attach one end of
each chain, beginning with the
longest and working in order to the
shortest. Close the jump ring.

6 Cut two 2–4-in. (5–10cm) pieces
of 2–3mm link chain. Attach a
chain to each of the hammered
jump rings.

7 On one end, use a 3–4mm jump
ring to attach a lobster claw
clasp and an end link. Repeat on
the other end, substituting a 2-in.
(5cm) piece of 4–5mm link chain
for the clasp.

9

8 On a head pin, string a crystal.
Make the first half of a wrapped
loop. Attach the end link of
extender chain and complete
the wraps.

9 Hang the hammered jump rings
on the pegs of a Chain Sta, or

use T-pins to secure the jump rings
to a foam board. Arrange the
nugget units as desired, frequently
checking the drape. Adjust the
placement of nugget units if
necessary. Complete the wraps on
each nugget unit.

Twist 2 Necklaces

by Deb Huber

String two long, individual strands and use a twister clasp to generate multiple style options. Have fun experimenting to discover your own style.

TECHNIQUES
One-four strands
- looping a single strand for a multistrand effect
- using a specialty clasp

SUPPLIES
1 yd. (.9m)
- **4** 16-in. (41cm) strands 6mm beads, in 4 colors
- **4** 8-in. (20cm) strands 6mm Czech glass beads, in 4 colors
- **20–40** 6–8mm flat spacers
- **20–40** 3mm round spacers
- flexible beading wire, .014 or .015
- **2** crimp beads
- **2** crimp covers
- twister clasp
- chainnose pliers
- diagonal wire cutters
- crimping pliers (optional)

1

2

3

4

1 Cut a piece of beading wire (Basics). String five to nine 6mm beads as desired. String a flat spacer.

2 String five to nine 6mm beads as desired. String a round spacer. String beads and spacers until the strand is within 1 in. (2.5cm) of the finished length.

3 On one end, string a crimp bead. String the remaining end through the crimp bead plus one more bead. Check the fit. Add or remove beads, if necessary.

Tighten the wire and crimp the crimp bead (Basics). Trim the excess wire. Use chainnose pliers to close a crimp cover over the crimp bead.

4 Make a second necklace. To wear the necklaces as a short rope necklace: String both necklaces on a twister clasp, twist the necklaces together, and string the other end of both necklaces on the clasp.

TIPS

• Twister clasps are also called tornado clasps or pearl shorteners.

• If you prefer, use waxed linen instead of bead wire and finish with a knot. A crimp cover can be used to hide the knot.

Design Alternatives

The clever use of the twister clasp allows for many variations on this necklace design.

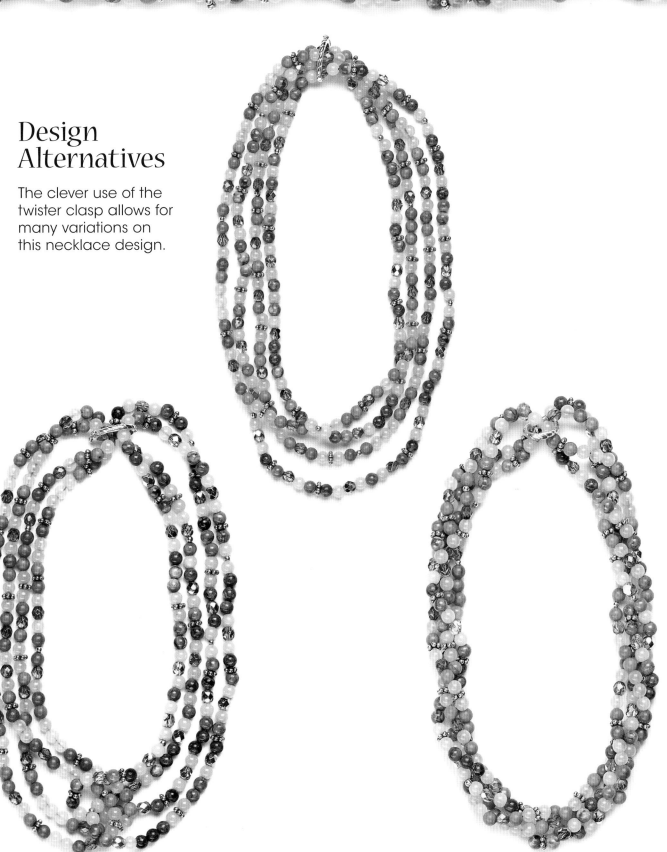

Spectrum Snapshot

by Anne Nikolai Kloss

With three strands of 6mm crystals, this bracelet's natural beauty is a triple treat. Three-hole spacer bars make it easy to keep the strands aligned, and three-to-one connectors provide a smooth and streamlined finish.

Secrets for Success

Choosing related hues unifies the strands of this bracelet, while the three-hole spacer bars divide the strands into distinct sections. See the Color Notes (p. 49) for suggestions.

Before crimping, shape the bracelet into a circle and fasten the clasp. This will ensure flexibility so that the strands are not too tight.

TECHNIQUES

Three strands

- using a three-strand clasp
- making connections between multiple strands

SUPPLIES

7 in. (18cm)

- **63 or more** 6mm round crystals, **21** or more in each of **3** colors: dark, medium, and light
- **6 or more** 4 x 15mm three-hole spacer bars
- **2** 4 x 15mm three-to-one connector bars
- **6** 3mm round spacers
- **6** 2mm round spacers
- flexible beading wire, .014 or .015
- **6** crimp beads
- toggle clasp
- **2** 4mm jump rings
- **2** pairs of chainnose pliers
- diagonal wire cutters
- crimping pliers (optional)

COLOR NOTES

PINKS
light: light rose
medium: rose champagne
dark: padparadscha

LIGHTER REDS
light: fire opal
medium: Indian red
dark: Siam

DARKER REDS
light: Indian red
medium: Siam
dark: garnet

BLUE-GREENS
light: chrysolite
medium: erinite
dark: tourmaline

PURPLES
light: violet AB
medium: tanzanite AB
dark: amethyst AB

BLUES
light: Indian sapphire
medium: Indian sapphire AB
dark: Pacific opal

YELLOW-GREENS
light: lime
medium: khaki
dark: olivine

BROWNS
light: jonquil
medium: light Colorado topaz
dark: smoked topaz

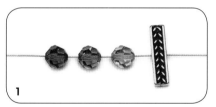

1

1 a Determine the finished length of your bracelet. Add 5 in. (13cm) and cut three pieces of beading wire to that length.
b On one wire, string a dark-colored crystal, a medium-colored crystal, a light-colored crystal, and the center hole of one spacer bar.

2

2 a Repeat the pattern in step 1b until the strand is within 2 in. (5cm) of the desired length, ending with a crystal.
b On each end, string a 3mm spacer, a crimp bead, a 2mm spacer, and the center loop of a three-to-one connector. Go back through the beads just strung. Do not crimp the crimp beads.

3

3 On the remaining wires, repeat steps 1b, 2a, and 2b, with the respective holes of the spacer and connector bars. Check the fit, and add or remove beads from each end if necessary. Crimp the crimp beads (Basics) and trim the excess wire. Open two jump rings (Basics) and attach each half of the clasp to the single loop on the connectors. Close the jump rings.

Time-Traveling Trendsetter

by Angela Bannatyne

Angela says she loves this piece because "it's relevant and current, but at the same time has a wonderful vintage feel." The multicolored beads make the necklace versatile. This project is a great way to use up your bead stash — chances are, you already have plenty of coordinated beads on hand.

TECHNIQUES

Three strands
- combining a single-strand back with a multistrand front
- using three-to-one connectors (see Design Alternative)

SUPPLIES

39 in. (.99m)
- 22mm oval faceted glass bead
- **3** 14mm (large) pearls
- **5** 12mm (small) pearls
- **4** 12mm crystal saucers
- **34** 8mm fire-polished beads
- **5** 7mm textured round metal beads
- **5** 8º seed beads
- **5** 4mm round spacers
- **3** 4mm flat spacers
- **5** 8mm bead caps
- 10 in. (25cm) ¼-in. (6mm) ribbon
- 73–76 in. (1.8–1.9m) chain, 6–10mm links
- **52** 2-in. (5cm) head pins
- **2** 16mm decorative jump rings
- 10mm jump ring
- chainnose pliers
- diagonal wire cutters
- roundnose pliers
- scissors

1

2

3

1 On a head pin, string a 12mm pearl, a bead cap, and a round spacer. Make the first half of a wrapped loop (Basics). Make five 12mm (small) pearl units. On a head pin, string a fire-polished or saucer bead. Make a plain loop (Basics). Make 34 fire-polished units and four saucer units. On a head pin, string an 8º seed bead and a 7mm metal bead. Make five metal-bead units. On a head pin, string a flat spacer and a 14mm pearl. Make a plain loop. Make three 14mm (large) pearl units.

2 Cut a 14-in. (36cm) piece of chain. Open the loop of a large-pearl unit (Basics) and attach the center link. Close the loop. On each side, within 4 in. (10cm) of the center unit, attach three large- and three small-pearl units.

3 Attach a metal-bead unit and seven to 10 fire-polished or saucer units between the pearl units.

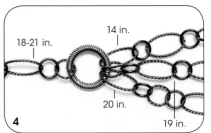

4 Cut three pieces of chain: 18–21, 19, and 20 in. (46–53, 48, and 51cm). Open a 16mm decorative jump ring (Basics) and attach an end link of the 18–21-in. 20-in., 19-in., and 14-in. chains, in that order. Close the jump ring. Repeat on the other ends of the chains.

5 On a head pin, string a 22mm bead. Make the first half of a wrapped loop. Cut a 2-in. (5cm) piece of chain. Attach the bead unit and complete the wraps.

6 Attach two fire-polished units to the dangle. Use a 10mm jump ring to attach a small-pearl unit, the dangle, a metal-bead unit, and the 16mm jump ring.

7 Cut a 10-in. (25cm) piece of ribbon. Tie a bow around a 16mm jump ring.

TIP
• Arrange the bead units on a bead board to balance the colors and sizes before attaching them to the chain.

Design Alternatives

There's room for endless adaptation of this basic one-in-back, three-in-front design. Connect three strands of beads on flexible beading wire to a single-strand chain back: Cathy Jakicic's strands of lampworked barrel beads and rondelles connect directly to the first link of chain, with crimp beads holding the wire in place, while Roxie Moede's dark pearls and rhinestones connect via three-to-one connectors.

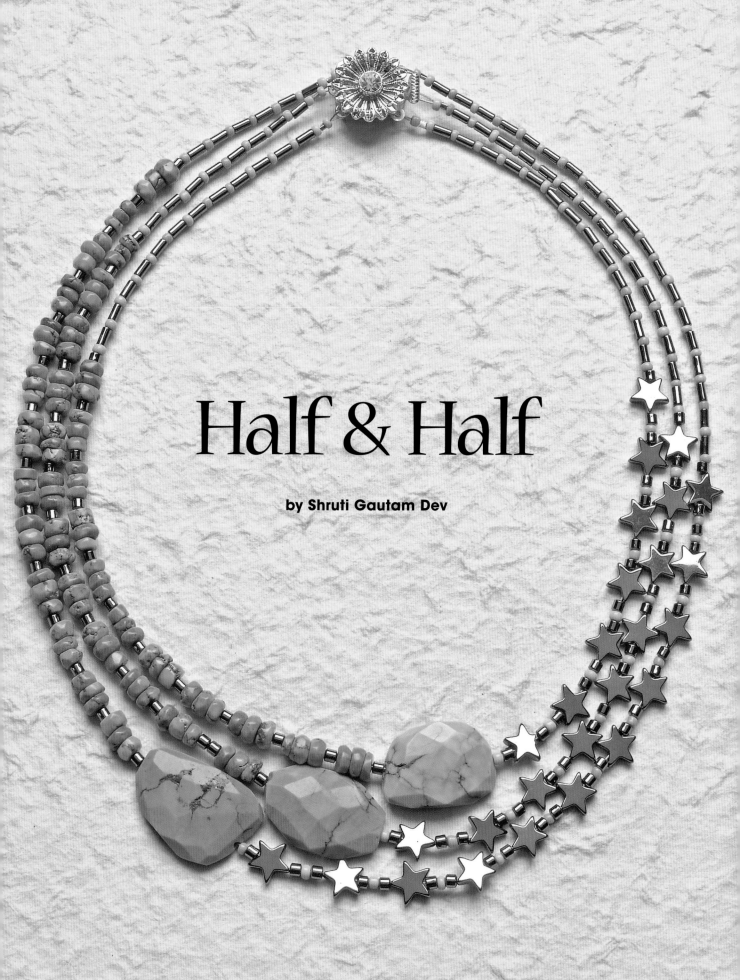

Half & Half

by Shruti Gautam Dev

Throw convention off-balance with an asymmetrical necklace. The two halves — geometric shapes and free-form chips — meet at off-kilter nuggets. Tapering to smaller beads at the back of the necklace creates a comfortable fit. You'll love the dramatic drape of these pieces.

Secret for Success

Start the innermost strand with a standard measurement, such as 16 or 18 in. (41 or 46cm), and add 6 in. (15cm) for finishing. Let the space between strands be determined by the size and shape(s) of the beads included in the design. Eyeball the drape or clasp the necklace before crimping the ends to ensure a comfortable space between the previous strand and the current strand.

TECHNIQUES

3 strand
- using a three-strand clasp
- staggering an asymmetrical pattern from strand to strand

SUPPLIES

16-20 in. (41-51cm)
- **3** nuggets, approximately 15 x 25mm
- **27** 8mm flat beads
- 16-in. (41cm) strand 5mm heishi beads or chips
- **73-130** 3-4mm beads

- 3g 8º seed beads or 16-in. (41cm) strand 2mm beads
- 2g 11º seed beads
- flexible beading wire, .014 or .015
- **6** crimp beads
- three-strand clasp
- chainnose or crimping pliers
- diagonal wire cutters

1

2

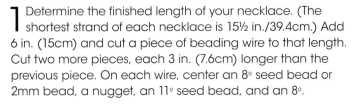

3

1 Determine the finished length of your necklace. (The shortest strand of each necklace is 15½ in./39.4cm.) Add 6 in. (15cm) and cut a piece of beading wire to that length. Cut two more pieces, each 3 in. (7.6cm) longer than the previous piece. On each wire, center an 8º seed bead or 2mm bead, a nugget, an 11º seed bead, and an 8º.

2 On one end of the shortest wire, string a flat bead, an 8º, an 11º, and an 8º. Repeat five times. String a flat bead and an 8º.

3 On the other end of the shortest wire, string three heishi beads or chips and an 8º. Repeat 10 times.

TIP

Keep the size of the nuggets in mind when you check the necklace's fit. For a flattering drape, allow more length between strands with wide nuggets. Strands with narrow nuggets can have less variation in length.

4 On one end of the middle wire, string the pattern in step 2 eight times. String a flat bead and an 8º. On the other end, string the pattern in step 3, and repeat 11 times.

5 On one end of the longest wire, string the pattern in step 2 ten times. String a flat bead and an 8º. On the other end, string the pattern in step 3, and repeat 12 times.

6 On each end of each strand, string an 8º and a 3–4mm bead. Repeat until each strand is within 1 in. (2.5cm) of the desired length. End with a 3mm bead.

7 Arrange the strands so the nuggets are staggered with the middle strand's nugget in the center. Check the fit, and add or remove beads from each end if necessary. Allow 1 in. (2.5cm) for finishing.

8 On each end, string an 11º, a crimp bead, an 11º, and the corresponding loop of half of the clasp. Go back through the beads just strung and tighten the wires. Crimp the crimp beads (Basics) and trim the excess wire.

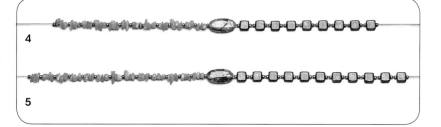

Lush & Lucky
by Brenda Schweder

1

2

3

1 Cut six pieces of beading wire (Basics). On each of two wires, string peridot beads until the strand is within 3 in. (7.6cm) of the finished length.

2 On the third wire, string an accent bead. String peridot beads on each end until the strand is within 3 in. (7.6cm) of the finished length, making sure that the accent bead is off-center.

3 On the fourth wire, string peridot beads, interspersing metal tube beads, until the strand is within 3 in. (7.6cm) of the finished length. Repeat on the fifth and sixth wires.

Multiple strands of grassy peridot get lucky in this design. The cones provide a tailored and smooth finish for the eclectic strands, and coordinate with the metal tube beads and good-luck charm for a unified look.

TECHNIQUES
Six strands
- finishing with cones
- using a focal bead on one strand only

SUPPLIES
7 in. (18cm)
- 20–25mm accent bead
- 20–25mm charm
- **12–16** 12mm metal tube beads
- **3** 16-in. (41cm) strands 5–9mm peridot beads
- **12** 2–3mm round spacers
- flexible beading wire, .014 or .015
- 7 in. (18cm) 22- or 24-gauge half-hard wire
- 6mm jump ring
- 4–5mm jump ring (optional)
- **12** crimp beads
- **2** cones
- hook clasp and **2** soldered jump rings
- chainnose pliers
- diagonal wire cutters
- roundnose pliers
- crimping pliers (optional)

Secrets for Success

When gathering multiple strands into a cone, be sure to arrange (or add) smaller beads near the ends of each strand. That way, the combined strands will taper down to the clasp both physically (the end beads won't fight for position) and aesthetically (the visual flow will be more appealing).

To make sure that the strands fall nicely, do not overtighten the wires. Double-check the fit before you crimp the crimp beads.

4 Cut a 3½-in. (8.9cm) piece of 22- or 24-gauge wire. Make a wrapped loop (Basics) on one end. On one side, on each beading wire, string a spacer, a crimp bead, and the loop. Repeat on the other side. Check the fit, allowing 2 in. (5cm) for the clasp. Add or remove beads, if necessary. Go back through the beads just strung and tighten the wire. Crimp the crimp beads (Basics) and trim the excess beading wire.

5 On each end, string a cone. Make the first half of a wrapped loop. Attach a soldered jump ring and complete the wraps. If necessary, open a 4–5mm jump ring (Basics) and attach the hook clasp and one of the soldered jump rings. Close the jump ring. (My clasp was already attached.)

6 Use a 6mm jump ring to attach a charm and one of the soldered jump rings.

Focus on Filigree

by Jennifer Gorski

1

1 String an accent bead or bicone crystal on a head pin. Make a wrapped loop (Basics).

2 Open a jump ring (Basics). Attach the bead unit and a loop of a filigree component.

2

Close the jump ring. Determine the finished length of your necklace. Divide that number in half, add 6 in. (15cm), and cut six pieces of beading wire to that length.

3

3 To make one side of the middle strand: On a wire, string a bicone, a crimp bead, and a middle loop of the component. Go back through the beads, tighten the wire, and crimp the crimp bead (Basics).

Design Alternative

A bracelet with a filigree centerpiece applies the same design principles and techniques as the necklace.

Using this filigree as a both a centerpiece and an anchor for the pearl and gemstone strands creates a balanced multistrand design. Positioning the pendant upside down creates a natural spot for a bead dangle — the perfect finishing touch.

Graduating each strand helps the necklace lie flat around your neck.

TECHNIQUES

Three strands
- using a multistrand clasp
- attaching strands to a centered focal piece

SUPPLIES

15 in. (38cm)
- filigree component, approximately 25mm
- 6–10mm accent bead (optional)
- **2** 16-in. (41cm) strands 4–5mm round pearls
- 16-in. (41cm) strand 4–5mm round faceted gemstones

- **19–31** 4mm bicone crystals
- flexible beading wire, .014 or .015
- 1½-in. (3.8cm) head pin
- 4mm inside diameter jump ring
- **12** crimp beads
- three-strand clasp
- chainnose and roundnose pliers
- diagonal wire cutters
- crimping pliers (optional)

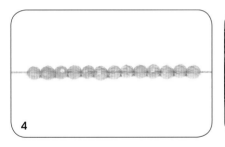

4

5

6

7

4 String faceted beads until the necklace is half the desired length.

5 To make one side of the top strand: On a wire, string a bicone, a crimp bead, and a loop of the component. Go back through the beads, tighten the wire, and crimp the crimp bead. String pearls until the necklace is half the desired length. Repeat to make one side of the bottom strand.

6 Repeat steps 3–5 on the other side of the pendant.

7 On each end, string a bicone, a crimp bead, a bicone, and the corresponding loop of half of the clasp. Go back through the beads just strung and tighten the wire. Check the fit, and add or remove beads if necessary. Crimp the crimp bead and trim the excess wire.

TIPS
- If the necklace component has an even number of loops, attach an additional jump ring between two of the loops in step 2.
- If you need extra length, incorporate more crystals in the necklace.

Gemstone
Twist

by Naomi Fujimoto

1

2

1 Cut three 12–14-in. (30–36cm) pieces of beading wire. On one wire, string a liquid silver bead and a top-drilled bead. Repeat until the strand is within 1 in. (2.5cm) of the finished length, ending with a liquid silver bead. String a second strand.

2 On the third wire, string a top-drilled bead and a liquid silver bead. Repeat until the strand is within 1 in. (2.5cm) of the finished length, ending with a liquid silver bead.

Top-drilled beads are often sold on strands with plastic tubes or wire coils in between. As Naomi was pondering her options with these amethyst and iolite strands, she twisted them together and wrapped them around her wrist. Just like that, a design was born! The liquid silver does double duty: It makes the project more budget friendly while also protecting the top-drilled beads from breakage.

Secret for Success

Crimp the crimp beads while the bracelet is in a curved position to allow each strand to drape properly. Crimping when the strands are straight may crowd the beads.

TECHNIQUES

Three strands

- connecting many strands to a single-strand clasp
- adding a twist

SUPPLIES

7 in. (18cm) with extender

- **3** 8-in. (20cm) strands 10–18mm beads, top drilled
- **30–40** 10mm liquid silver beads
- **4** 5–6mm large-hole spacers
- flexible beading wire, .014 or .015
- 3 in. (7.6cm) 24-gauge wire
- **2** crimp beads
- lobster claw clasp
- 1½-in. (3.8cm) chain for extender, 9–10mm links
- chainnose pliers
- diagonal wire cutters
- roundnose pliers
- crimping pliers (optional)

3

4

TIP

- To make minor adjustments in the length of each strand, substitute 6mm liquid silver beads for the 10mm ones on the ends.

3 On one side, over all three wires, string a spacer, a crimp bead, a spacer, and a lobster claw clasp. Repeat on the other side, substituting a 1½-in. (3.8cm) piece of chain for the clasp. Check the fit, and add or remove beads if necessary. Go back through the beads just strung and tighten the wires. Crimp the crimp beads (Basics) and trim the excess wire.

4 Cut a 3-in. (7.6cm) piece of 24-gauge wire. String a top-drilled bead and make a set of wraps above it (Basics). Make the first half of a wrapped loop (Basics). Attach the end link of chain and complete the wraps.

by Mary
Champion

A New Slant on Bails

1 Cut a 6-in. (15cm) piece of 20-gauge wire. On one end, make a plain loop (Basics). String: 5mm spacer, oval bead, bail, oval, bail, oval, bail, oval. Make a plain loop.

2 Close a crimp cover over the bottom loop.

3 Cut three 12-in. (30cm) pieces of beading wire. On each wire, string a crimp bead and the top loop. Go back through the crimp

bead and tighten the wire. Crimp the crimp bead (Basics).

4 Over the crimps and the loop, close a crimp cover. Over all three wires, string a large-hole spacer. On each wire, string

This necklace features economical gemstone chips and an ingenious alternative use for pendant bails. Using crimp covers at the connection points provides a smooth transition, a tidy finish, and a unified design.

TECHNIQUES
Three strands
- using a multistrand clasp
- incorporating bails

SUPPLIES
20 in. (51cm)
- **4** 18mm oval beads
- 16-in. (41cm) strand 6–10mm chips
- 8g 11º seed beads
- 6–9mm large-hole spacer
- 5mm spacer
- **3** 3–4mm round spacers
- **3** 6mm bails

- flexible beading wire, .014 or .015
- 6 in. (15cm) 20-gauge half-hard wire
- **12** crimp beads
- **10** crimp covers
- three-strand clasp
- chainnose pliers
- diagonal wire cutters
- roundnose pliers
- crimping pliers (optional)

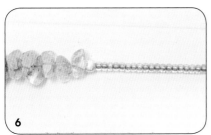

7–8 in. (18–20cm) of 11º seed beads.

5 Cut a 14-in. (36cm) piece of beading wire. String a crimp bead and the loop of a bail. Go back through the crimp bead and tighten the wire. Crimp the crimp bead. Close a crimp cover over the crimp. String 3–4 in. (7.6–10cm) of chips.

6 a String a 3–4mm spacer and 4–5 in. (10–13cm) of 11ºs. **b** Repeat steps 5 and 6a with the remaining bails.

7 On each side, on each wire, string a crimp bead and a loop of half of a clasp. Check the fit, and add or remove beads if necessary. Go back through the last few beads strung and tighten the wire. Crimp the crimp bead and trim the excess wire.

8 Close a crimp cover over each crimp.

Gilded Cuff

by Cathy Jakicic

COLOR NOTES

The Crystallized Swarovski pearl colors are deep brown, brown, bright gold, and rosaline. Cathy bought the three gold-toned pearl colors on multicolored strands, and used one and a half 16-in. (41cm) strands of the golds and half a strand of the rosaline pearls. The paste colors are violet and patina.

Five strands of gold-toned and soft lavender pearls are a perfect foundation for a supersized gilded filigree flower. Applying the gilder's paste is as easy as finger painting. Add a bit of color to the bead caps to pull the whole look together.

TECHNIQUES

Five strands

- using memory wire
- using a focal on one strand only

SUPPLIES

2½ in. diameter (6.4cm)

- 50mm brass filigree flower
- **85–100** 10mm crystal pearls, in four colors
- **42–50** filigree bead caps
- oval bracelet-diameter memory wire
- 1½-in. (3.8cm) decorative head pin
- chainnose and roundnose pliers
- diagonal wire cutters
- heavy-duty wire cutters
- gilder's paste, in two colors
- soft cloth

1 Use heavy-duty wire cutters to cut a piece of memory wire five coils long. On one end, make a loop with roundnose pliers.

2 Use your fingers to apply gilder's paste to the bead caps and filigree flower, leaving some areas ungilded. Allow the paste to dry. Buff the caps and filigree with a soft cloth.

3 String three pearls, a bead cap, a pearl, and a bead cap. Repeat until the bracelet is half the desired length.

4 On a decorative head pin, string a pearl and the filigree. Make a wrapped loop (Basics).

5 String the filigree. String the pearl pattern from step 2 until the bracelet is the desired length. Make a loop at the end of the memory wire.

String a Crystal Sonnet

by Linda Hartung

There's one simple way to add strands to your neckwear — just wear additional necklaces in coordinating designs, so no one will ever know the two pieces aren't connected. The shorter necklace here is a true multistrand piece that features three strands and a crystal-encrusted clasp that can be worn as a focal piece in front. Want to make it a four-strand collar? Layer an adjustable crystal chain over the shorter necklace to end with a flourish of color and a dramatic Y dangle.

Secret for Success

Depending on the clasp you choose for the three-strand necklace, you may have to adjust the chain lengths. A wider or narrower clasp could make the graduated chains hang differently.

TECHNIQUES

Four strands
- using a three-strand clasp
- adding an extra strand

SUPPLIES

three-strand necklace, 17 in. (43cm)
- 16mm three-tier crystal button
- 50 in. (1.3m) navette crystal chain, 10 x 5mm links
- **6** 4mm jump rings
- rotunda clasp
- chainnose and roundnose pliers, or **2** pairs of chainnose pliers
- diagonal wire cutters
- two-part epoxy

Y-necklace, 22 in. (56cm)
- 22mm teardrop pendant
- **3** 16mm teardrop pendants
- **3** 11 x 5mm briolettes
- 22 in. (56cm) navette crystal chain, 10 x 5mm links
- 1½-in. (3.8cm) crystal head pin
- **4** 6mm jump rings
- **4** 4mm jump rings
- lobster claw clasp
- chainnose pliers
- diagonal wire cutters
- roundnose pliers

COLOR NOTES

crystal chain links: fuchsia, padparadscha, rose, light peach, rose
water opal briolettes: padparadscha
16mm teardrops: ruby, light rose
22mm teardrop: ruby

three-strand necklace

1 Mix two-part epoxy and apply a layer of glue to the clasp. Set the button in the clasp and allow to dry.

2 Cut a 16-in. (41cm) piece of chain. Cut a second piece one link longer than the first. Cut a third piece two links longer than the first. Make sure each chain begins and ends with a crystal link (not a ring).

3 Use a jump ring to attach each end of a chain to each side of the clasp. Repeat with the remaining chains, attaching them in graduating length to the clasp's corresponding loops.

Y-necklace

1 Cut a 22-in. (56cm) piece of chain. Make sure the chain ends with a crystal link on one end and a ring on the other. Use a 4mm jump ring to attach a lobster claw clasp and the end crystal link (directions continued on page 68).

TIP

If you have bentnose pliers, you can use them to grip the loop in the final step in making the pendant bail. If you're new to wire wrapping, the bentnose pliers may be more comfortable to use.

5

Repeat step 4 on the next link. Make sure to attach the briolette and teardrop units on alternate sides as shown.

4

Use a 4mm jump ring to attach a briolette and the next ring in the chain. Use a 6mm jump ring to attach a 16mm teardrop and the ring.

3

Use a 4mm jump ring to attach a briolette and the 6mm jump ring from step 2. Use a 6mm jump ring to attach a 16mm teardrop and the jump ring.

2

Make a teardrop pendant with bail. Use a 6mm jump ring (Basics) to attach the teardrop unit to the remaining end of the chain.

Technique: Teardrop pendant with bail

1 On a crystal head pin, string a 22mm teardrop pendant. Leaving ⅛ in. (3mm) between the head of the head pin and the teardrop, bend the wire upward. About ⅛ in. (3mm) above the top of the teardrop, bend the wire back at a 45-degree angle.

2 Place the jaws of your roundnose pliers above the bend and pull the wire over your pliers to create a curve.

3 Reposition the jaw of your pliers to the other side of the curve. Squeeze and rotate the pliers to complete the loop. Bend the wire tail away from the pendant.

4 Holding the base of the loop with one set of pliers, wrap the wire a little more than one full rotation behind the head of the head pin. Trim the excess wire.

Amazing Greys

by Linda Hartung

While shades of grey usually suggest uncertainty, the style of this sophisticated necklace is a sure thing. A white-to-black range of pearls and crystals float on 12 smoky WireLace strands in a remarkably lightweight necklace.

1 Decide how long you want your necklace to be. Double that measurement, and cut six strands of WireLace to that length. Cut a 6-in. (15cm) piece of WireLace. Use it to tie an overhand knot (Basics) at the center of the six strands. Fold them in half and apply glue to the knot.

2 Twist the end of each of the 12 strands to form a point (apply glue to the point if necessary). Leaving a ½-in. (1.3cm) gap in the center of the strands for a pendant, string the pearls and crystals on the strands as shown, staggering the pearls and crystals. Repeat the pattern until you have three strands of each pearl color. Apply glue next to each bead and slide the bead over the glue.

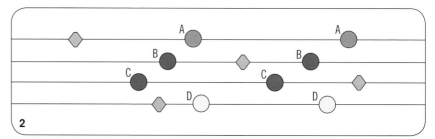

3 Gently pull the beaded strands together, making them even. Cut a 6-in. (15cm) piece of WireLace and use it to tie an overhand knot 1 in. (2.5cm) from the end of the strands. Apply glue to the knot.

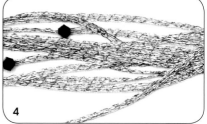

4 On one side, trim the excess WireLace close to the knot. Prepare two-part epoxy and fill a bell end-cap half full. Insert the knot in the cap and let it dry. Repeat on the other end.

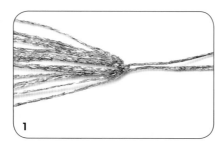

5 Center a pendant on the strands.

6 On each end, open the loop of the bell cap (Basics) and attach half of a clasp.

COLOR NOTES

WireLace: titanium
Pearls: white, light grey, dark grey, black

3mm bicone crystals: jet hematite AB2X
6mm bicone crystals: jet hematite

TECHNIQUES

12 strands

- gathering strands in a bell cap or bead tip
- centering a pendant over all strands

SUPPLIES

17 in. (43cm)

- 35mm filigree pendant with bail
- **24** 4mm glass pearls, in four colors
- **12** 3mm bicone crystals
- 6 yd. (5.5m) 1mm WireLace

- **2** bell end-caps
- box clasp
- chainnose pliers
- G-S Hypo Cement
- two-part clear-drying epoxy

Design Alternative

For a softer look, choose different colors of WireLace and white pearls and crystals. Omit the pendant, if desired.

Fiesta necklace

by Rebecca Conrad

Be ready to rumba when the next party comes around. Gather a gemstone go-go pendant and a hank of multicolored seed beads, then intersperse larger round beads for pops of navy, turquoise, and red to balance the size of the pendant. Your festive 12-strand necklace will have you looking salsa-smart in no time.

Secret for Success

With 12 strands to fill with tiny seed beads, this necklace could take forever — there are about 4,000 11º seed beads on a hank. Consider using a time-saving bead spinner. It will be necessary to unthread the needle each time you add a larger bead. It's well worth the extra trouble to add some beads of different sizes.

TECHNIQUES

12 strands
- finishing with cones
- centering a pendant over all strands

SUPPLIES

20 in. (51cm)
- 45–50mm gemstone go-go pendant
- **4–8** 9mm round beads
- **12–16** 7mm round beads
- **32–38** 5mm round beads
- 10g 8º multicolored seed beads
- hank 11º multicolored seed beads, matte finish
- flexible beading wire, .014 or .015
- 6 in. (15cm) 22-gauge half-hard wire
- **2** 6mm jump rings
- **2** cones
- **24** crimp beads
- S-hook clasp
- chainnose pliers
- roundnose pliers
- diagonal wire cutters
- bead spinner (optional)
- crimping pliers (optional)

1 Cut 12 pieces of beading wire (Basics). On one wire, string 11º seed beads, interspersing 8º seed beads and 9mm round beads, until the strand is within 3 in. (7.6cm) of the finished length.

2 On each of three wires, string 11ºs, interspersing 8ºs and 7mm rounds, until each strand is within 3 in. (7.6cm) of the finished length.

3 On each of six wires, string 11ºs, interspersing 8ºs and 5mm rounds, until each strand is within 3 in. (7.6cm) of the finished length.

4 On each of two wires, string 11ºs, interspersing 8ºs, until each strand is within 3 in. (7.6cm) of the finished length. Center a go-go pendant over all 12 strands.

5 Cut a 3-in. (7.6cm) piece of 22-gauge wire. On one end, make a wrapped loop (Basics). On one side of each beaded strand, string a crimp bead, an 11º, and the loop. Repeat on the other side. Check the fit, and add or remove beads if necessary. Go back through the beads just strung and tighten the wires. Crimp the crimp beads (Basics) and trim the excess wire.

6 On one end, string a cone. Make a plain loop (Basics). Open a jump ring (Basics) and attach the loop and an S-hook clasp. Close the jump ring. Repeat on the other end, omitting the clasp.

Design Alternative

Here's an earthy option: loop four twisted strands of beads through an oval gold horn donut.

Petals & Pearls Cuff

by Naomi Fujimoto

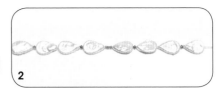

COLOR NOTE

bicone crystals: black diamond satin

1 Cut three pieces of beading wire (Basics). On one wire, center two to eight 11º seed beads. On each end, string two pearls, a bicone crystal, and two pearls.

2 On another wire, center two to eight 11ºs. On each end, string: pearl, bicone, two pearls, bicone, pearl. Repeat on the third wire. These are the outer strands.

3 On each end of each wire, string a bicone, a crimp bead, and the corresponding loop of half of a clasp. Check the fit, and add or remove beads if necessary (see Tips, p. 75). Go back through the beads just strung and tighten the wire. Crimp the crimp bead (Basics) and trim the excess wire.

4 Pin a flower over the 11ºs.

Wrist corsages aren't just for prom — floral cuffs make a pretty and charming accessory. To create your own, string several rows of flat petal-shaped pearls as a backdrop for a fabric flower. If you want more focus on the strands of pearls, just use a smaller flower.

Secret for Success

This bracelet is designed as a three-strand, but the beauty of multistrand jewelry is that you're always able make a piece more delicate or more substantial. For a daintier bracelet, string only two rows of pearls and attach a 60mm flower.

TECHNIQUES
Three strands
- centering a focal bead over all strands
- using a multistrand clasp

SUPPLIES
7 in. (18cm)
- 60–70mm fabric flower with pin back
- **2** 16-in. (41cm) strands 15–17mm flat teardrop pearls
- **16–22** 3mm bicone crystals
- 1g 11º seed beads
- flexible beading wire, .012 or .014
- **6** crimp beads
- three-strand clasp
- chainnose or crimping pliers
- diagonal wire cutters

TIPS
• There are about 24 pearls on each strand. Though the Supply List calls for two strands, you may be able to complete the project with only one strand, depending on your wrist size. If you opt to buy two strands, you should have pearls left to make matching earrings.
• If you have trouble stringing .014 beading wire back through the 3mm bicones, you can finish with 3mm spacers instead.

• When adjusting the length of each strand, add or remove seed beads at the center of the bracelet. Though it might seem like extra work to unstring the pearls and crystals to get to them, it won't take long to restring.
• If you like vintage styles, pin a brooch to the bracelet. You can use any brooch you like, as long as the pin back is large enough to fit over the seed beads.

3

On each end, string: bead cap, spacer, 1¼ in. (3.2cm) liquid silver beads, crimp bead, corresponding loop of a five-strand clasp (see Secret for Success). Check the fit, and add or remove beads if necessary. Go back through the beads just strung, tighten the wire, and crimp the crimp bead (Basics). Trim the excess wire.

Cut a 19–23-in. (48–58cm) piece of beading wire. Cut four more pieces, each 2 in. (5cm) longer than the previous piece. On each wire, string 12 round beads (Tip, below).

1

On the shortest wire, string a bead cap, ¾ in. (1.9cm) of heishi beads, and a bead cap. String rounds until the strand is within 3 in. (7.6cm) of the finished length. Repeat on the remaining wires, stringing each heishi section about ¼ in. (6mm) longer than the previous one.

2

TIP
If you use smaller or larger beads for this project, you'll need to adjust the number of beads used in step 1.

Inspired by Opposites

by Meredith Jensen

Asked to design jewelry based on the idea of balance, Meredith was initially stumped — it's easy to find inspiration in a flower or other object, but designing a piece of jewelry based on a word or idea is an entirely different task. The resulting necklace demonstrates balance in contrary elements throughout an asymmetrical, multistrand design: The balance between calm and hyper colors, organic and polished stones, and a natural and elegant style coalesced into a unified, fashionable design.

TECHNIQUES

Five strands
- placing an asymmetrical focal point
- using a multistrand clasp

SUPPLIES

20 in. (51cm)
- 16-in. (41cm) strand 7mm heishi beads or rondelles
- **5** 16-in. (41cm) strands 6mm round beads
- **50–60** 4–6mm liquid silver beads
- **10** 2–4mm spacers
- **20** 4mm bead caps
- flexible beading wire, .014 or .015
- **10** crimp beads
- five-strand box clasp
- chainnose or crimping pliers
- diagonal wire cutters

Design Alternatives

For a bracelet with matching colors and sizes, you can stagger the focal beads rather than grouping them as in the necklace. Or, try flipping the proportion of rondelles and round beads.

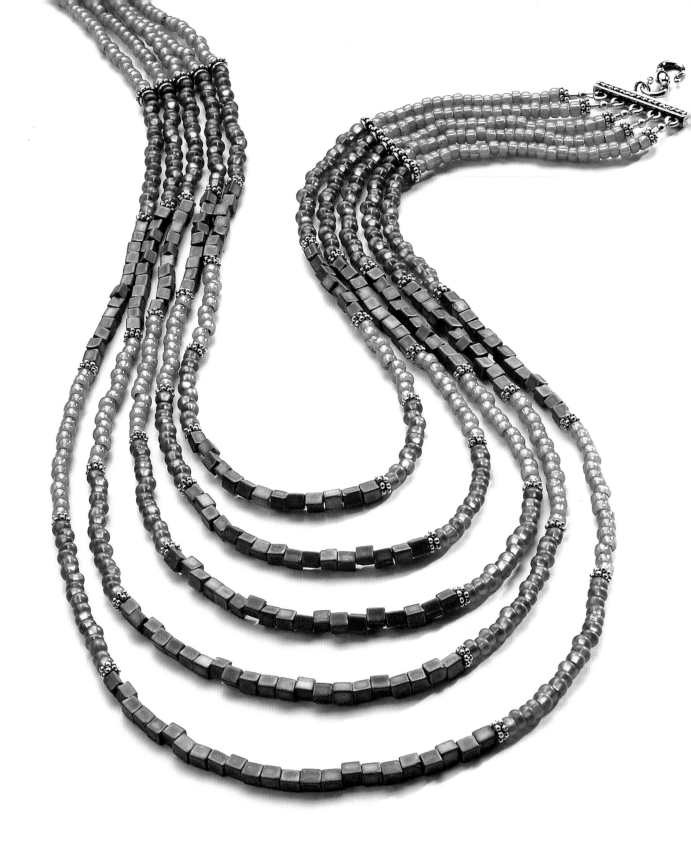

Dramatic Drape

by Anne Nikolai Kloss

Create a graduated five-strand necklace with perfect alignment by following Anne's "Secrets for Success" and careful instructions. A bead design board is a key tool for this project: Because the board's channels are curved, each strand will be in proportion, giving the necklace an even, graceful drape.

Secrets for Success

There are two ways to ensure uniform bead spacing: count the number of beads, or measure the length strung.

Miyuki and Toho both manufacture seed beads that are consistent in size. Other seed beads can be more irregular, throwing off your alignment if you rely on counting the beads.

Crimp the crimp beads while the necklace is curved into your preferred drape. Crimping when the strands are straight will crowd the beads.

TECHNIQUES
Five strands
- using connector bars and a single-strand clasp
- aligning a pattern

SUPPLIES
17–26 in. (43–66cm)
- 60g 6º or 8º seed beads, 30g each of matte and another finish
- 30g 4mm Japanese cube beads
- 2 6 x 27mm five-strand spacer bars
- 2 10 x 27mm five-to-one connector bars
- 100 4mm flat spacers
- 10 3mm round spacers
- flexible beading wire, .014 or .015
- 10 crimp beads
- 2 in. (5cm) chain, 4–5mm links
- 2 5mm jump rings
- S-hook clasp
- chainnose or crimping pliers
- diagonal wire cutters
- 2 rulers
- bead design board with at least five channels

1 Determine the finished length of your necklace. Add 6 in. (15cm) to the shortest measurement and cut a piece of beading wire to that length. Cut four more pieces, each 2 in. (5cm) longer than the previous wire. Align a ruler along each 2-in. (5cm) mark on the design board. String cubes on the shortest wire,

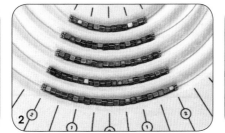

filling in the design board's top channel between the rulers. String cubes on each successive wire; the longest wire will have the most cubes.

2 String two flat spacers on each end of each wire.

3 Align a ruler along each 4-in. (10cm) mark on the design board. String matte beads on each end of each strand, filling in the channels between the rulers. String two flat spacers on each end of each strand.

4 Align a ruler along each 6-in. (15cm) mark on the design board. String silver-lined beads on each end of each strand, filling in the channels between the rulers. String two flat spacers on each end of each strand.

5 Align a ruler along each 8-in. (20cm) mark on the design board. String cubes on each end of each strand, filling in the channels between the rulers. String two flat spacers on each end of each strand.

6 String 2 in. (5cm) of matte beads on each end of each strand. On each end, string the respective hole of a five-strand spacer bar.

7 String 2 in. (5cm) of silver-lined beads on each end of the shortest strand. On the next strand, string that amount plus one bead. On the remaining strands, string one bead more than on the previous strand. String two flat spacers on each end of each strand.

8 On each strand, string a crimp bead, a round spacer, and the respective loop of a connector bar. Go back through the beads just strung plus a few more and tighten the wires. Check the fit, and add or remove an equal number of beads from each end if necessary. Crimp the crimp beads (Basics) and trim the excess wire.

9 Open a jump ring (Basics). Attach one connector bar's loop and the clasp. Close the jump ring. Cut a 2-in. (5cm) piece of chain. Attach a jump ring to the chain and the remaining connector bar's loop. Close the jump ring.

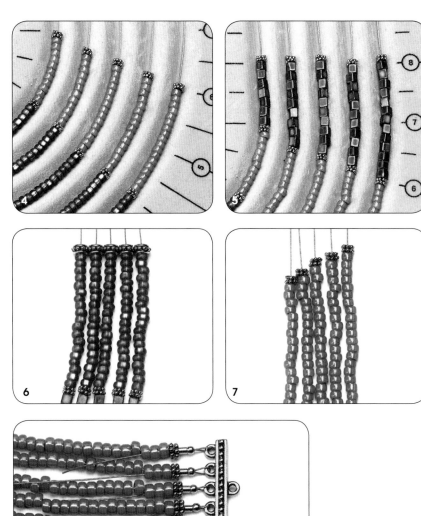

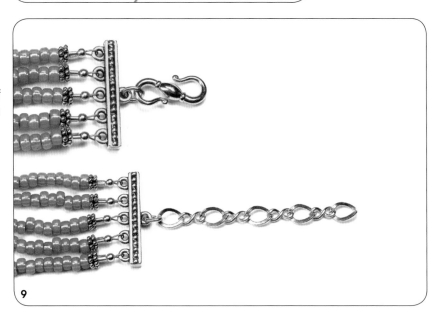

A Beader's Prerogative

by Cathy Jakicic

1 Cut a 24–26-in. (61–66cm) piece of beading wire. String chips interspersed with 6mm and 4mm fire-polished beads until the strand is within 2 in. (5cm) of the finished length.

2 On each end, string a crimp bead and a soldered jump ring. Go back through the last few beads strung. Tighten the wire and crimp the crimp bead (Basics).

3 Make the connectors (p. 82). Remove the watch pendant from the chain. Cut one 3-in. (7.6cm), two 2-in. (5cm), and two 5-in. (13cm) pieces from the chain. Open the loops of the connectors and attach the chains. Close the loops as you go. Use a 4mm jump ring to attach a soldered jump ring to each end.

4 Cut a 26–29-in. (66–74cm) piece of beading wire. String 6mms interspersed with chips and 4mms until the strand is within 2 in. (5cm) of the finished length. Follow step 2.

5 Center the pendant on the strand.

6 Cut a 34–37-in. (86–94cm) piece of beading wire. String teardrop beads, chips, 6mms, and 4mms until the strand is within 2 in. (5cm) of the finished length. Follow step 2.

Turn a collection of coordinating strands into nearly endless wardrobe options with a no-commitment-necessary clasp that allows you to change strands as you change your mind. Just finish the strands with jump rings, and slip them on and off the clasp to vary your look.

Secret for Success

A necklace created with strands of different styles could easily become busy or clash, so, make sure there's a common element (even a subtle one) in all strands to hold your composition together.

TECHNIQUES

Four strands
- creating a necklace with an adjustable strand count
- using a specialty clasp

SUPPLIES

20–28 in. (51–71cm)
- **2** 8-in. (20cm) strands 16mm teardrop beads, top drilled
- 32-in. (81cm) strand 8–12mm gemstone chips
- **3** 8-in. (20cm) strands 6mm round Czech fire-polished beads
- 8-in. (20cm) strand 4mm round Czech fire-polished beads
- watch pendant on 24-in. (61cm) chain

- flexible beading wire, .014 or .015
- **8** 7mm soldered jump rings
- **2** 4mm jump rings
- **4** 2-in. (5cm) eye pins
- **6** crimp beads
- multistrand clasp
- chainnose pliers
- diagonal wire cutters
- roundnose pliers
- crimping pliers (optional)

connectors • On an eye pin, string a 4mm fire-polished, a 6mm fire-polished, and a 4mm. Make a plain loop (Basics). Make four connectors.

1 attaching the clasp • Open the loops of half of a clasp. Attach one end of each strand, from longest to shortest, to one loop, pushing the strands toward the clasp's hinge.

2 Close the loops and center the strands over both loops. Repeat with the other half of the clasp.

3 The weight of the strands will keep the jump rings centered when the necklace is worn.

TIP

Adjust the length of individual strands by adding jump rings to each end.

Design Alternatives

With four strands, you can make style combinations for
every occasion and mood.

by **Andrea Marshal**

Blooming Inspiration

1

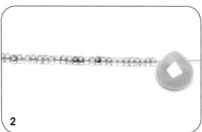

2

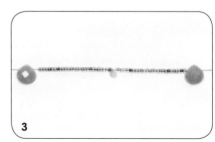

3

Peruvian opals and Swiss topaz mix warm and cool blue tones in this necklace. The steady drizzles of blue or silver seed beads interspersed with beautiful briolette drops are just one version of an easily adaptable design. Even "if you don't have the exact materials," Andrea says, "you can still make something beautiful."

Secret for Success

One of the trickiest part of stringing a multistrand necklace is lining up all the elements — which makes this design perfect! It works best as an asymmetrical necklace, with the briolettes spaced at uneven intervals.

TECHNIQUES

Four strands
- connecting many strands on a single-strand clasp

SUPPLIES

18 in. (46cm)
- 16-in. (41cm) strand 14–18mm (large) briolettes
- 8-in. (20cm) strand 4–5mm (small) briolettes
- 15–20g 8° seed beads
- **8** 4mm spacers
- flexible beading wire, .014 or .015

- **2** 4–5mm jump rings
- **2** 4–5mm soldered jump rings
- **8** crimp beads
- box clasp
- chainnose and roundnose pliers, or **2** pairs of chainnose pliers
- diagonal wire cutters
- crimping pliers (optional)

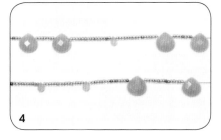

4

1 Cut four pieces of beading wire (Basics). On one wire, center a large briolette.

2 On each end of the first wire, string 3 in. (7.6cm) of seed beads and a large briolette. Repeat until the strand is within 2 in. (5cm) of the finished length.

3 On the second wire, center a large briolette. On each end, string 2 in. (5cm) of seed beads, a small briolette, 2 in. (5cm) of seed beads, and a large briolette. Repeat until the strand is within 2 in. (5cm) of the finished length.

4 On the remaining two wires, string briolettes and seed beads as desired until each strand is within 2 in. (5cm) of the finished length.

5 On each side, over each wire, string a spacer and a crimp bead. Over all four wires, string a soldered jump ring. Check the fit, and add or remove beads if necessary. Go back through the last few beads strung and tighten the wires. Crimp the crimp beads (Basics) and trim the excess wire.

6 On one side, open a jump ring (Basics) and attach the soldered jump ring and half of a clasp. Close the jump ring. Repeat on the other side.

TIP

Use Wire Guardians if you are stringing heavy briolettes; they will lend greater support to your piece.

5

6

TIPS
• String seed beads not only in different colors, but in different cuts. The silver necklace uses bugle beads for one strand.
• For even more variety, consider using accent beads in different shapes.

Design Alternative

While the blue-and-silver necklace on p. 84 has a delightfully uneven array of briolettes, designer Naomi Fujimoto drew inspiration from the mix of materials and created a symmetrical alternative. Naomi's version uses triangles rather than briolettes, and keeps the drops to one strand only.

Contributors

Angela Bannatyne lives in Orlando, Fla., with her husband, two daughters, and one big dog. She says her biggest beading challenge is not having exactly the right beads for a piece and having to improvise — proving that you can never have enough beads! Contact her at renegadegirl1@aol.com, or visit avenuea.etsy.com.

Ute Bernsen is married with two grown children and lives in Carlsbad, Calif. An artist, silk painter, meditation teacher, and jewelry designer, she is creating a course that combines beading or painting with meditation. Contact her at ute@silkpaintingisfun.com.

Mary Champion has been creating bead art for over seven years. Her work ranges from jewelry to beaded dolls and more! Mary's art can be found in stores and galleries from Seal Beach to Laguna Beach, Calif., or at her website, championbeadedart.com.

Rebecca Conrad has won several awards for her jewelry designs. She is a member of the Loose Bead Society of Milwaukee, Wis. Contact Rebecca at bjc1941@aol.com.

Shruti Gautam Dev is a mixed-media jewelry artist who creates her own jewelry components and lampworked beads in her studio in India. She has been making jewelry since 2001. Visit artyzenworld.com, or contact Shruti at shrutigdev@gmail.com.

Naomi Fujimoto is Senior Editor of *Bead Style* magazine and the author of *Cool Jewels: Beading Projects for Teens*. Contact her at nfujimoto@ beadstyle.com, or visit her blog at cooljewelsnaomi.blogspot.com.

Jennifer Gorski creates jewelry from her home in the Rocky Mountains of Colorado. Jewelry inspirations often come to her in the middle of the night while sleeping. Contact Jennifer at djgorski@comcast.net.

Michelle Gowland is a jewelry artist who resides with her dogs near the beautiful and inspirational Hilton Head Island, S.C. Her work has been published in multiple magazines, as well as seen on the runways of New York's Fashion Week and the red carpet of the 2009 Emmys. Contact her at mdgdesigns@hargray.com or visit mdgdesigns.etsy.com.

Linda Hartung is co-owner of Alacarte Clasps™ and WireLace®, and a designer/teacher and Ambassador for CREATE YOUR STYLE with SWAROVSKI ELEMENTS. Her designs and techniques have been featured on the television show Beads, Baubles, and Jewels, as well as in many beading and jewelry-making publications around the world. Contact her at linda@alacarteclasps. com, or visit alacarteclasps.com or wirelace.com.

Deb Huber started beading about 16 years ago and started her business, Clever Treasures, in 2004. Her theory is to create quick, easy and fun pieces. Visit her online at clever-treasures.com.

Cathy Jakicic is Editor of *Bead Style* magazine and the author of the book *Hip Handmade Memory Jewelry*. She has been creating jewelry for more than 15 years. Contact her via email at cjakicic@beadstyle.com.

Brightly colored stones are **Meredith Jensen's** beading material of choice. Her favorite place to buy them: the Bead&Button Show, held each June just a few miles from her home in Milwaukee, Wis. Contact Meredith via her website, m-jewelry.net.

Anne Nikolai Kloss is a bead artist and instructor from Waukesha, Wis. Contact her at annekloss@mac.com.

Addie Kidd is a former associate editor of *Art Jewelry* magazine. Contact her in care of Kalmbach Books.

Jane Konkel is Associate Editor of *Bead Style* magazine, and contributed several new designs to the book *Bead Journey*. Contact her via e-mail at jkonkel@beadstyle.com.

Andrea Marshall left a career in real estate to devote herself to jewelry making in 2005. She sells her work in boutiques, galleries, department stores, and most recently on cruise ships. Contact her at andrea@ andreagems.com or visit andreagems.com.

Brenda Schweder is the author of the books *Junk to Jewelry*, *Vintage Redux*, and *Iron Wire Jewelry*, and has contributed to *Bead Style*, *Bead&Button*, and *Art Jewelry* magazines as well as many of Kalmbach Publishing Co.'s other special issues. Contact her at b@brendaschweder.com, or visit brendaschweder.com.

With her mother, **Karli Sullivan** co-owns Confetti: The Bead Place, a bead store in Surprise, Ariz. Contact her at (623) 975-7250, via email at madredolce@yahoo.com, or on her website at confettibeads.com.

Helene Tsigistras' jewelry has been featured in *Bead Style* and *Bead&Button* magazines. She has also contributed her designs to several books, including *Easy Birthstone Jewelry*. Contact her via email at htsigistras@kalmbach.com.

Express your style with quick & easy projects!

Fast, fabulous, and fun projects await you in the *Easy Beading* series. Collected from the pages of *Bead Style* magazine, the 75+ projects in each volume (an incredible value!) use easy techniques to showcase crystals, gemstones, pearls, glass, metal, **and more!**

You'll find:

- A handy beading glossary and Basics section to eliminate guesswork
- An array of techniques so you can learn something new
- Varied project styles that appeal to every taste and budget
- Dozens of design alternatives for extra practice
- And much more!

$29.95 each